CRAIG G. BARTHOLOMEW AND MICHAEL W. GOHEEN

THE **TRUE STORY** OF THE WHOLE WORLD

finding your place
in the biblical drama

FAITH
ALIVE®
Christian Resources

Grand Rapids, Michigan

The True Story of the Whole World: Finding Your Place in the Biblical Drama © 2004 by Craig G. Bartholomew and Michael W. Goheen. Originally published in English under the title *The Drama of Scripture* by Baker Academic, a division of Baker Book House Company, Grand Rapids, Michigan 49516, U.S.A. All rights reserved.

This edition published by Faith Alive Christian Resources, 2850 Kalamazoo Ave. SE, Grand Rapids, MI 49560. Printed in the United States of America.

We welcome your comments. Call us at 1-800-333-8300 or e-mail us at *editors@faithaliveresources.org.*

Library of Congress Cataloging-in-Publication Data
Goheen, Michael W., 1955-
The true story of the whole world: finding your place in the biblical drama / Michael Goheen and Craig Bartholomew.
      p.   cm.
Originally published: The drama of Scripture / Craig G. Bartholomew and Michael W. Goheen. Grand Rapids, Mich.: Baker Academic, c2004.
    ISBN 978-1-59255-476-8 (alk. paper)
    1. Bible—History of Biblical events. I. Bartholomew, Craig G., 1961- .
II. Bartholomew, Craig G., 1961- . Drama of Scripture. III. Title.
    BS635.3.G64   20009
    230'.041—dc 22

                                                                 2008055608

10 9 8 7 6 5 4 3 2 1

To Mike's parents Ross and Rilyne Goheen for
their faithfulness in passing on this story in life,
deed, and word.

To Craig's father Leonard Bartholomew for his
lifelong support.

Contents

Preface

A few years ago Bob Webber and Phil Kenyon issued a passionate and clarion call to the evangelical community. It was a summons to growing faithfulness to the gospel in the midst of huge threats. After affirming the authority of Scripture and noting the myriad of global challenges facing the evangelical church at the beginning of the twenty-first century they say, "Today, as in the ancient era, the Church is confronted by a host of master narratives that contradict and compete with the gospel. The pressing question is: Who gets to narrate the world?"[1]

They believe, and rightly so, that if the Christian Church is to be faithful in the midst of competing stories, this question must be answered unequivocally in terms of the biblical narrative: *The Bible tells the true story of the world.* Thus their first section is called "On the Primacy of Biblical Narrative." Getting this straight is the crucial starting point. The following sections on the Church, theology, worship, spiritual formation, and the believer's life in the world are all tied to the biblical story. The Church finds its identity in the role it plays in the biblical story; theology deepens our understanding of this story; worship enacts and tells this story; spiritual formation equips the Church to embody this story; and the believer's life in the world, including all of public life, is a witness to the truth of this story.

Our passion is similar: that people learn to read the Bible as it was meant to be read—as the true story of the world. *The True Story of the Whole World* has been written to tell the biblical story of redemption as a unified, coherent narrative of God's ongoing redemptive work in the world. After God had created the world, and after human rebellion had corrupted it, God set out to restore the whole world: "While justly angry, God did not turn away from a world bent on destruction but turned to face it in love. With patience and tender care the Lord set out on the long road of redemption to reclaim the lost as his people and the world as his kingdom."[2] The Bible narrates the story of God's journey on that long road of restoration. It is a unified and progressively unfolding drama of God's action in history for the salvation of the whole world. The Bible is not a mere jumble of history, poetry, lessons in morality and theology, comforting promises, guiding principles, and commands; it is fundamentally coherent. Every part of the Bible—each event, book, character, command, prophecy, promise, and poem—must be understood in the context of the *one* story line.

This book is our *telling* of that story. We invite the reader to make it their story, to find their place in it, and to *indwell* it as the true story of our world.

There are three important emphases in this book. First, we stress the comprehensive scope of God's redemptive work: the biblical story does not move toward the destruction of the world and our individual "rescue" to heaven. It culminates in the restoration of the entire creation and all of human life to its original goodness.

Second, we emphasize our place within the biblical story, that is, the era of biblical history in which we live. Some refer to four questions as foundational to a biblical worldview: "Who am I?" "Where am I?" "What's wrong?" "What's the solution?" N. T. Wright adds an important fifth question: "What time is it?"[3]—that is, "Where do *we* belong in this story? How does it shape *our* lives in the present?" We will explore the biblical answers to these five questions as part of our telling of the grand story of the Bible.

Third, we highlight the centrality of *mission* within the biblical story. The Bible narrates *God's mission* to restore the creation. *Israel's mission* flows from this: God chose a people to again embody God's creational purposes for humanity and so be a light to the nations, and the Old Testament narrates the history of Israel's response to their divine calling. *Jesus' mission* unfolds when he comes on the scene, taking on himself the missionary vocation that had been Israel's. Jesus embodies God's purpose for humanity and accomplishes the victory over sin, opening the way to a new world. When his earthly ministry is over, he leaves his Church with the mandate to continue in that same mission. And so the *Church's mission* is our central task: in our own time, standing as we do between Pentecost and the return of Jesus, we as the people of God are to witness to the rule of Jesus Christ over all of life.

We have also borrowed from N. T. Wright his very helpful metaphor of the Bible as a drama.[4] But whereas Wright speaks of *five* acts—creation, sin, Israel, Christ, church—we tell the story in terms of *six* acts. Following Brian Walsh and Richard Middleton we add the coming of the new creation as the final act of the biblical drama.[5] We have also added a Prologue. This Prologue addresses in a preliminary way what it means to say that human life is shaped by a story.

This is the third version of our book first published by Baker Academic Press (Grand Rapids, Mich., 2004) and SPCK (London, 2006). This Faith Alive version is slightly revised from the SPCK edition. The main title has been changed from *The Drama of Scripture* to *The True Story of the Whole World*, but the subtitle, *Finding Our Place in the Biblical Story* has remained the same. This new title reflects what Michael Goheen would often tell his first year biblical theology students at the beginning of the semester: "This course is about the true story of the world."

This edition is suitable as a study version for individuals and churches. Three things distinguish both the SPCK and Faith Alive editions from the original Baker publication. First the book has been significantly shortened. Many of the details in the earlier book have been eliminated. Second, almost all of the explanatory footnotes have been dropped. Third, each "Act" is followed by a section on the contemporary significance of that part of the story. These sections are intentionally brief and by no means exhaustive; rather they are meant to suggest how the acts may be read with integrity in terms of their significance for today. These sections are followed by some questions that can be used as discussion starters to reflect on the meaning of the story for our lives today.

There is a website that accompanies this book (www.biblicaltheology.ca). It provides various resources that may help you to use this book: course syllabus, adult Bible study class schedules of various lengths, PowerPoint slides, more study questions, articles, links, and more.

We are deeply grateful that so many have found the Baker and SPCK versions of this book to be helpful; it has been used beyond our wildest expectations in many settings and in many countries. And it makes us even more grateful to those who contributed to the original project. They include Fred Hughes and Alan Dyer from Britain, Dawn Berkelaar, Gene Haas, and Al Wolters from Canada, Wayne Kobes from the United States, and Wayne Barkhuizen from South Africa. Jim Kinney from Baker Academic Publishing and Alison Barr from SPCK were very helpful and encouraging on the first two editions. And now we are grateful to Len Vander Zee from Faith Alive Christian Resources who has made this shorter study edition available in North America. Undoubtedly, the one to whom we are most indebted is our friend Doug Loney, Dean of Arts and Humanities and Professor of English at Redeemer University College. Doug has given to the original manuscript and then to the SPCK volume much time and skill as a writer, helping make it a lively and coherent text. His sterling work continues to be reflected in this new Faith Alive version.

Craig G. Bartholomew, Hamilton, Ontario
Michael W. Goheen, Burnaby, British Columbia

Prologue

Alasdair MacIntyre offers the following example to show how particular events can only be understood in the context of a story.[1] He imagines himself at a bus stop when a young man standing next to him says, "The name of the common wild duck is *histrionicus, histrionicus, histrionicus.*" We understand the meaning of the sentence. But why on earth is he saying it in the first place? This particular action can only be understood if it is placed in a broader framework of meaning. Three stories could make this particular incident meaningful. The young man has mistaken the man standing next to him for another person he saw yesterday in the library who asked, "Do you by any chance know the Latin name of the common duck?" Or he has just come from a session with his psychotherapist who is helping him deal with his painful shyness. The psychotherapist urges him to talk to strangers. The young man asks, "What shall I say?" The psychotherapist says, "Oh, anything at all." Or again, he is a foreign spy who has arranged to meet his contact at this bus stop. The code that will reveal his identity is the statement about the Latin name of the duck. The meaning of the encounter at the bus stop depends on which story shapes it: in fact, each story will give the event a different meaning.

This is also true of human life. In order to make sense of our lives and to make our most important decisions, we depend on the story that provides the broader framework of meaning for our lives. Again MacIntyre says it well: "I can only answer the question, 'What am I to do?' if I can answer the prior question, 'Of what story do I find myself a part?'"[2] Our lives, and the questions and events that fill them, take their meaning from within some larger story.

The story in which I find significance and purpose might be simply the story of my life, my private biographical journey. But it's likely to be broader than this: the story of my family or my town—even of my country and my civilization. The more deeply I probe for meaning, the larger the context I will seek. And this leads to a very important question: Is there a true story of the whole world in which I am called to live my life? Lesslie Newbigin puts it this way: "The way we understand human life depends on what conception we have of the human story. What is the real story of which my life story is part?"[3] Is there a "real story" that provides a framework of meaning for all people in all times and places, and therefore for my own life in the world?

Many people today have abandoned the hope of discovering such a "real story." They argue that a true account of the world cannot be found, that individuals and communities must be content with the meanings to be discovered in the more modest and limited stories of their personal lives. In addition, a commitment to pluralism in our culture often implies that we should not even look for any such overarching story, one that could be true for all people, all communities, all nations—for to find such a thing would imply that not all stories are equally valid.

Yet there are many others who do claim that there is one true and real story that gives meaning to all people and all communities. Muslims, for example, believe that their story (told in the Quran) is the true story of Allah, his creation of the world, his rule over history, and his final triumph. One day, says the Muslim, all people will see that this is the one true story. Similarly, the modernist committed to the story that emerged in the Enlightenment believes that humankind will ultimately conquer nature by the application of human reason alone, and that science and technology will help us build a better world for all. This story shapes the lives and outlook of many people in Western Europe and North America.

Christians too believe that there is one true story: the story told in the Bible. It begins with God's creation of the universe and human rebellion and runs through the history of Israel to Jesus and on through the Church, moving to the coming of the kingdom of God. At the very center of this story is the man called

Jesus of Nazareth, in whom God has revealed his fullest purpose and meaning for the world. Only this one story unlocks meaning of human history—and thus the meaning of your life and mine.

This kind of grand story provides us with an understanding of the whole world and of our own place within it. It's a big story that encompasses and explains all the smaller stories of our lives. Implicit in this claim is the idea that "a story . . . is . . . the best way of talking about the way the world actually is."[4]

Such a comprehensive story gives us the meaning of not merely personal or national history, but of universal history. The Muslim, the modernist, and the Christian each believes that his or her story alone is the true story of the world, that either the Quran, or the Enlightenment story of human progress, or the Bible will ultimately be acknowledged by all to be true. But these stories cannot all be uniquely true. We must choose.

We realize how difficult it is to hear this in the midst of a society that has tacitly adopted the philosophy of pluralism. Pressure for harmony among cultures and nations urges us to regard the Bible as just another volume in the world's library of interesting stories, of which perhaps none—or all—might be more or less reliable. But to do so would be to pretend that the Bible is something other than what it claims to be: the one true story of the world. According to the biblical narrative, the meaning of our whole world's history finds its meaning and purpose in the person of Jesus. We may either embrace that story as true or reject it as false, but we must not simply reshape the Bible to suit our own preferences. The Bible's claim to tell the one true story of our world is central to its meaning.

Sadly, many Christians have not recognized this essential character of the Bible. A Hindu scholar of world religions once said to Newbigin,

> I can't understand why you missionaries present the Bible to us in India as a book of religion. It is not a book of religion—and anyway we have plenty of books of religion in India. We don't need any more! I find in your Bible a unique interpretation of universal history, the history of the whole of creation and the history of the human race. And therefore a unique interpretation of the human person as a

responsible actor in history. That is unique. There is nothing else in the whole religious literature of the world to put alongside it.[5]

His complaint was that even Christian missionaries to India had not recognized the Bible for what it is. Instead, they reduced it to the status of just one more book of religion. This Hindu scholar recognized that there is nothing quite like the Bible in the whole religious literature of the world.

Why have Christians, who claim to believe the Bible, not seen what treasure they have? The problem is that Christians, even Christian scholars, break the Bible up into little bits: historical bits, devotional bits, moral bits, theological bits, narrative bits. In fact, it has been chopped into the kind of fragments that fit into the nooks and crannies of the Enlightenment story! When this is allowed to happen, the Bible forfeits its claim to be the one comprehensive, true story of our world. It is held captive within the other story—the humanist narrative. And that other story will shape our lives.

N. T. Wright has said, "The whole point of Christianity is that it offers a story which is the story of the whole world. It is public truth."[6] We agree—and that's why we have written this book, which seeks to tell the story of the Bible as a whole, coherent drama. We invite you to come along with us. You may be a Christian who wants to understand your story better. Or you may have other reasons to be interested in understanding what this book, one that has had such a formative influence on Western culture, is all about. In any case, we invite you to come along with us on a journey in which we claim that God is acting in history for the salvation of the world.

We have adopted N. T. Wright's very helpful metaphor of the Bible as a drama. While he speaks of the Bible as a five-act play, we employ a six-act structure. We also adopt what we believe to be the most comprehensive image found in Scripture, that of the kingdom. The outline follows:

Act 1: God Establishes the Kingdom—Creation
Act 2: Rebellion in the Kingdom—Fall
Act 3: The King Chooses Israel—Redemption Initiated
    Scene 1: A People for the King
    Scene 2: A Land and a King for God's People
Interlude: A Kingdom Story Waiting for an Ending—The Intertestamental Period

Act 4: The Coming of the King—Redemption Accomplished

Act 5: Spreading the News of the King—The Mission of the Church

   Scene 1: From Jerusalem to Rome

   Scene 2: And into All the World

Act 6: The Return of the King—Redemption Completed

We believe this to be the true story of the world. And we invite you to find your place in it.

Finding Our Place in the Story[7]

1. In this Prologue we have tried to show how individual events have meaning only when they are understood in the context of a story. Here's an exercise to test that idea.

   Imagine this scene: a florist delivers a beautiful bouquet to a woman at her doorstep. When she reads the card that comes with the flowers, she faints dead away.

   What stories can you think of that would give this simple action several different meanings?

2. Most modern secular people assume that there is one basic story of the world. What would the outline of this story look like if it were expressed as the answers to these questions?

   - *Who am I?* What does it mean to be human?
   - *Where am I?* Where did our world come from?
   - *What is wrong?* Why does the world seem to be so troubled?
   - *What is the remedy?* Can humans alone fix the problems of the world?

3. How would a Christian begin to answer the same four questions?

4. What are the biggest differences between a secular and a Christian worldview?

5. Why do you think so many Christians have adopted some (or all) of a secular worldview? What can we do to ensure that our view of the world is consistent with what we say we believe?

6. What is the danger of "breaking the Bible into little bits"? Have you seen examples in devotionals, Bible studies, sermons or elsewhere? How can we prevent this from happening?

Act 1

God Establishes the Kingdom—**Creation**

Who Is the "LORD God"?

The biblical story opens with the words "In the beginning God . . ." That certainly signals immediately who the main actor is here. But who is this God? The names used for God in the opening chapters of Genesis tell us a lot about who he is. It probably doesn't matter too much to you that "Michael" is a Hebrew name meaning "(he) who is like God" or that "Craig" is a Gaelic word that means "a rocky outcrop." Although names are important in our culture, we do not often attach special meaning to them. But in the Old Testament world we are preparing to visit, the meaning of names bears great significance—and none more so than the names for God in Genesis and other Old Testament books.

In Genesis 1, the Hebrew word *Elohim* (translated simply as "God" in English Bibles) is the general name used for God throughout the ancient Near East. The Bible says that "God" brings the whole creation into existence out of nothing. But in Genesis 2:4, the biblical writers introduce another name for God. "God" is now called "the LORD God" (*Yahweh Elohim*). This highly unusual way of referring to God reveals some important things about who he is.

God reveals himself to Moses as *Yahweh* (Ex. 3; 6:1-12) when he calls Moses to lead the people of Israel out of slavery in Egypt. God chooses the name *Yahweh* to identify himself as the divine Redeemer, the God who rescues people from slavery and meets with them at Mount Sinai (Ex. 19:4).

When the names *Yahweh* (LORD) and *Elohim* (God) are linked together, as they are in Genesis 2:4, it makes the powerful point that the same God who rescues Israel from slavery has also made all things: this God is the Creator of heaven and earth. The Israelites first come to know God (through Moses) as their Redeemer; only afterward do they learn of God's role as the Creator.

It's not so different for us, even though we live so much further along in the biblical story. When we first come to know God through the saving work of his Son, Jesus, we meet him as our Savior and Redeemer. But soon we realize that God (Father, Son, and Holy Spirit) is also the Creator of all that was, or is, or shall be: he is the one eternal LORD God, *Yahweh Elohim*. Thus the minute we start to witness to our faith and to tell the Christian story (as the bigger story in which our personal story belongs), we inevitably begin at the start of it all: the Creation itself. "In the beginning, God . . ."

A Faith for Israel

The first act of any drama is worth paying attention to, and the first act of the biblical drama is no exception. The early chapters of Genesis, telling the story of creation, were written long ago in a culture quite different from our own. Though some aspects of the creation stories in Genesis 1 and 2 may seem strange to us, we need to remember that they made perfect sense to the people of Israel when they first heard them. This is because the writer uses imagery and concepts familiar to the people of his day. When we read the first chapters of Genesis against the backdrop of the ancient world in which they were written, we begin to see powerful messages we didn't recognize before.

Several scholars have pointed out a strong argumentative aspect to Genesis 1 and 2. Ancient Near Eastern people told many competing accounts of how the world came into existence. The Israelites undoubtedly heard these stories when they were captive in Egypt and also in Canaan when they began to settle there. It would have been all too easy for the Israelites to adopt the stories of those who lived in the land before them or alongside them and who (after all) supposedly knew the land much better than they did. Many of the gods worshiped by the Canaanites were closely associated with the fertility of the land. The newcomers struggling to learn how to farm there would be tempted to call out to these "gods" rather than to the LORD God.

We know quite a bit about the creation stories circulating in the ancient world. It is fascinating to see how the story told in Genesis 1 and 2 deliberately contradicts certain important elements of these stories. For example, look at how Genesis 1:16 describes the sun and the moon. The text does not refer to the sun by its normal Hebrew name but instead as "the greater light" God made for the day. Similarly, it calls the moon "the lesser light." Why? Probably because the sun and moon were so often worshiped as gods by the people among whom the Israelites were now living. In the Genesis story, readers cannot mistake the sun for a divinity to be worshiped; rather it is a created object placed in the heavens for the simple, practical purpose of providing light and heat. The Scripture places all the attention on the One who created this marvelous light, the One whose power is so great that by merely uttering a word, an entire universe springs into being. No mere "light" in the heavens is worthy of our worship. God alone is divine; God alone is to be worshiped. The whole of creation is pronounced "very good" (Gen. 1:31) because the One who has created it is good and infinitely superior to anything he has made.

> **The biblical story describes this world as a marvelous home prepared for humankind, a place in which men and women and children may live and thrive and enjoy the intimate presence and companionship of the Creator himself.**

This transcendent Creator is nothing like the fickle and selfish gods described in (for instance) the Babylonian creation story, who make humankind merely to serve as servants to wait on them and keep them happy. In Genesis, the God who creates the world places men and women within it as the crowning touch of all he has brought into being. The biblical story describes this world as a marvelous home prepared for humankind, a place in which men and women and children may live and thrive and enjoy the intimate presence and companionship of the Creator himself.

What Kind of Literature Is Genesis 1?

The creation stories of Genesis aren't merely descriptive, they're argumentative. They claim to tell the truth about the world, flatly contradicting other such stories commonplace in the ancient world. Israel was constantly tempted to adopt these other stories as the basis of its worldview in place of faith in the Lord God, who created the heavens and the earth.

But the Genesis creation narrative is more than an argument against other ancient world-making stories. It also aims to positively shape how we think about the world God has made and how we should live in it. It does so by telling a story. And we need to be sensitive to this story form if we are not to misinterpret it.

In order to understand the Genesis story of creation we must understand something about the kind of writing it is. Scholars themselves have a hard time describing this. But what they agree on is that the story told in the first chapters of Genesis has been very carefully crafted. So we need to focus as much on the way in which the story is told as on the details themselves. Some read these details as a modern historian or scientist would read them, as descriptions of actual events. Others read the stories more as polemical and poetic depictions of the mysterious inauguration of history itself. But however we read it, the broad outlines of the Genesis story are certainly as clear to us as they were to those who first heard it.

- God is the divine source of all that is.
- God stands apart from all other things in the special relationship of Creator to creation.
- The creation of humankind is the high point of all God's work of making and forming.
- God intended a very special relationship between himself and human beings.

In these chapters we are told the story of creation—but not to satisfy our twenty-first-century curiosity concerning the details of how God made the world. The Genesis story offers us something even more

The opening act of the Genesis drama proclaims the truth about God, about humankind, and about the world.

important—a true understanding of the world in which we live, its divine Creator, and our own place in it.

Over against the pagan religious notions dominant in Egypt and Canaan, the opening act of the Genesis drama proclaims the truth about God, about humankind, and about the world. It introduces us to the main actors in the play—God and humanity—and the world in which the historical drama will unfold.

The God Who Brings All Things into Being

Reading the first chapter of Genesis is rather like visiting a really great art exhibition. Suppose you are sitting quietly, overwhelmed by the beauty and power of the magnificent paintings. Someone approaches you and says, "Would you like to meet the artist?" Who could resist such an invitation! Genesis 1 is an introduction to the artist. And what an introduction it is! The first three words of the Hebrew Bible may be translated as follows: (1) "in the beginning"; (2) "[he] created"; (3) "God" (acting subject). These three short Hebrew words transport us back to the origin of everything, to the mysterious, personal source of all that is: the eternal, uncreated God. This God, who has no beginning and no end, merely speaks a word of command in order to bring into being everything else that exists.

The Genesis story emphasizes that creation was *spoken* into being. The idea of creation by the *word* of God preserves the radical distinction between Creator and creature. The story absolutely prevents us from considering creation as some kind of overflow of God's divine nature. There is no room for the idea that God and creation are somehow one. Instead, creation is a product of God's personal will. The only continuity between God and the creation is God's word.

Genesis 1 introduces us to God as the infinite, eternal, uncreated person who brings the whole of creation into existence. The "heavens and the earth" (v. 1) refers to the whole of creation. Light and darkness; day and night; sea and sky and land; plants, animals, and humankind—all come from God's powerful and good activity of creation. As the renowned Old Testament scholar Gerhard von Rad says, "The idea of creation by the word expresses the knowledge that the whole world belongs to God."[1] This is truly one of the points through which logic can barely wade, whereas faith can swim.

In Revelation 4:11, the throne room of God echoes with continual worship for God's work in creation:

> "You are worthy, our Lord and God,
> to receive glory and honor and power,
> for you created all things,
> and by your will they were created
> and have their being."

This hymn of praise in the last book of the Bible reiterates the profound truth about God implied from the beginning of the creation account in Genesis. By causing the creation to come into being by his word of power, God establishes it as his own vast kingdom. He is the great King over all creation, without limits of any kind, and is therefore worthy to receive all glory, honor, and power.

Ancient Near Eastern people knew all about authority. Tribal or national rulers enjoyed nearly absolute power. In a variety of ways, Genesis 1 pictures God as the Monarch, the royal one whose sovereignty extends by right and by power over the whole of creation. The slightest word of a mortal king in the ancient world carried the weight of a command. But this immortal King speaks, and by the divine command and plan the whole of creation springs into existence.

In the act of creating, God names what he creates, a further expression of sovereignty. "The act of giving a name meant, above all, the exercise of a sovereign right. . . . Thus the naming of this and all subsequent creative works once more expresses graphically God's claim of lordship over the creatures."[2]

In Genesis 1, God's word of command, the repeated phrase "Let there be . . ." brings into existence a creation characterized by precision, order, and harmony:

> Just as God is the One who sets time in motion and set up the climate,
> he is likewise responsible for setting up all other aspects of human
> existence. The availability of water and the ability of the land to grow
> vegetation; the laws of agriculture and the seasonal cycles; each of
> God's creatures, created with a role to play—all of this was ordered
> by God and was good, not tyrannical or threatening.[3]

God's creation is "good," and this creaturely goodness mirrors the Creator's own incomparable goodness, wisdom, and justice. God alone is the wise King over the great kingdom of all that is.

As King, however, God does not hold himself distant from the creation. God is not the sort of monarch who rules from afar and takes no interest in his territories or subjects. God reigns over the kingdom in a deeply personal way. God's words do not merely command; they also express his own involvement in the making of the cosmos. This can be seen in the mysterious phrase "Let us make human beings . . ." (1:26), which we take to be God addressing the heavenly council of angels. At this climactic moment, the text highlights God's own personhood and desire that there should be other entities distinct from (and yet related to) himself.

This desire finds dramatic expression as God blesses the humans he has made and speaks to them directly: "Be fruitful and increase in number; fill the earth and subdue it" (1:28). Here we see the personal relationship between the divine King and his human subjects. God invites these human creatures to participate in the great task of filling and ordering the world he has given them for their home. God's personal relationship with humankind is pictured even more clearly in Genesis 2 and 3. The LORD God (*Yahweh Elohim*) walks in the garden with Adam and Eve and shows the most intimate, personal concern for them and for their needs and responsibilities.

Humankind as God's Image

The creation of humankind brings to a climax the Genesis story of creation (1:26-28). In the biblical story by which we live, men and women are creatures designed and made by God. However we relate the creation to scientific theories, if we live by the biblical story we cannot think of ourselves merely as the random products of time and chance (as do advocates of atheistic evolution). Human beings are creatures of God, and according to Genesis (and the rest of the Bible), each human being is a special creature at that.

What makes humankind so special? God speaks personally with human beings—they enjoy a uniquely personal relationship with him. As Augustine observed long ago in his *Confessions*, we are made for God, and our hearts are restless until we find our rest in him. Genesis 3:8 stunningly evokes this relationship between the creating God and human creatures. Men and women are made for intimate relationship with God, and our creatureliness and earthiness present no obstacle to that relationship. God walks regularly with Adam and Eve in the huge garden he has set aside for them. The Creator discusses with them how this great garden

> Men and women are made for intimate relationship with God, and our creatureliness and earthiness present no obstacle to that relationship.

is developing and how its plants and animals are flourishing under their care.

Genesis 1 looks at humankind in its relationship to the world. Genesis 2 focuses on the man and the woman in their relationships to one another and to God. The two passages use different images and metaphors because they focus on different aspects of what it means to be human.

In Genesis 1:26-28 humankind is created in God's image, in God's likeness. Note that the words "image" and "likeness" make the same point. Though God is the infinite Creator, and humans are merely part of God's finite creation, there is something fundamentally similar between them. The "image" metaphor draws our attention to the striking similarity between humans and God without denying that we are radically different from God. If humankind is created "in God's image," then in some way we are like the One who created us. The following verses clarify that likeness.

In Genesis 1:26, God says, "Let us make human beings in our image . . . so that they may *rule* . . . over all the creatures." God then says to the human beings he has created, "Be fruitful and increase in number; fill the earth and subdue it. Rule . . ." (1:28). This phrase clarifies the fundamental similarity between God and humanity: humankind's unique vocation to rule over the non-human parts of creation on land and in sea and air, under God as the supreme Ruler over all.

God has assigned humanity the special role of serving as "under-kings" or stewards in the kingdom. We are to rule over the creation in order to enhance God's reputation and glorify God's name within God's cosmic kingdom.

Genesis 1:26-28 has become notorious among some environmentalists who believe this teaching has been used to justify much of the environmental destruction in the modern world. But however it may have been misinterpreted in the past, this passage clearly identifies humankind's vocation of rule or dominion over creation not as tyrannical exploitation of nature but as careful stewardship. God acts for the good of the creation and not for selfish pleasure. God creates a perfect home for humankind, and at every point in God's work, Genesis describes the creation as "good" and "very good." Over this good creation, God calls the human "ruler" to serve as steward or under-sovereign, to embody God's own care for and protection of the creation in his own sovereign rule over the earth. Psalm 8:6 expresses this wonderfully: the glory of human beings is that God has made them "rulers over the works of [his] hands." It is impossible to read this as suggesting that humans are free to do what they like with God's workmanship. Above all things, human caretakers are accountable to the divine Creator for the world entrusted to their care.

God gives humankind huge freedom and clear responsibility. Thus a better way of expressing the concept of humanity's "dominion" over creation may be to say that we are God's royal stewards, put here to develop the hidden potential in God's creation so that the whole of it may celebrate God's glory.

Imagine that you are a fifteenth-century sculptor and one day receive an e-mail from Michelangelo himself, asking if you would be willing to come to his studio to complete a piece of work he has begun. Your job is to continue the work in such a way that Michelangelo's own reputation will be enhanced by the finished product! God's call to us to "have dominion" over creation entails this sort of confidence in what we are capable of achieving. It also brings a heavy responsibility for what results from that stewardship. If this is what being "in the image of God" involves, then clearly our service for God is as wide as the creation itself, and it includes taking good care of the environment.

Theologians have often used the term "cultural mandate" or "creation mandate" when referring to these verses. Culture isn't just what appears on the walls of hushed museums or plays or music from the stages of concert halls. Culture is making something of the world. The biblical story of human beginnings calls us to bring every kind of cultural activity within the service of God. Indeed, there is a dynamic element to "the image of God." We "image" God in creation precisely as we develop its potential and cultivate its possibilities in agriculture, art, music, commerce, politics, scholarship, family life, church, leisure, and so on, in ways that honor God. As we develop the potential of God's creative command "Let there be . . . ," we continue to spread the goodness of God's creating work throughout the world.

Genesis 1 describes humankind as stewards ruling *coram deo*, that is, before the presence of God. The nature of our relationship finds expression in how we look after God's good creation. And we do this not merely as individuals, but as partners.

In Genesis 1, God makes humans "male and female." So God's imagebearers are always male or female, man or woman. This created gender distinction means that we always stand in relationship to one another as well as in relationship to God. None of us can be fully human on our own: we are always in a variety of relationships. Humans are made for God. Genesis 2 brings this and the other relationships in which humans live out their lives into sharper focus.

One of the ways Genesis expresses Adam's rule is in his naming of the animals. Just as God named the creation (in Genesis 1) as he formed it, here God invites Adam to name the animals God has made. Adam thus has one relationship to God and another to the animal world. But Adam needs more companionship than the animals provide. Genesis 2:18-25 tells us that God created Eve as a suitable helper and companion for Adam. Adam's exultant cry "This is now bone of my bones and flesh of my flesh" captures the joy of human companionship, and Adam and Eve's "one flesh" union (2:24) illuminates their physical and emotional intimacy. God demonstrates deep love for the human couple by providing what is best for them.

Adam and Eve's call to rule the creation manifests itself in their responsibility to work in the garden and care for it (2:15). As described in Genesis 2:8-14, this "garden" is more like a national park than one of our household gardens. It's criss-crossed by large rivers and swarming with all kinds of flora and fauna. Think of Adam and Eve as the first farmers and conservation officers. Once more it's clear that to be human involves a deep involvement with the earth by exploring its potential and caring for it. We are made for God. We are also made for one another. And we are made to care for the creation and to work within it.

The World as God's Kingdom

Though Christianity has often been accused of being otherworldly, it should be clear by now that the biblical story does not encourage anyone to feel detached from or superior to this world of space and time and matter. The Bible depicts the created, material world as the very theater of God's glory. It is the kingdom over which God reigns. These early chapters of Genesis call us to a very positive attitude toward the world. Though it is created (and therefore must never be put on the same level as the uncreated God), it is always described as "good." The repetition of the word "good" throughout Genesis 1 reminds us that the whole creation comes from God and that in its initial state it beautifully reflects God's own design and plan for it. Creation's bountiful diversity—light and darkness; land and sea; rivers and minerals; plants, animals, birds, and fish; human beings both male and female—all suggest the marvelous harmony of created things. Like an orchestra, it produces a symphony of praise to the Creator.

Genesis also reveals that our world exists within time. God creates the day and the night, and he names them. Because creation exists in time, God clearly intends for humans to develop what he has made. The man and the woman are to produce children from their one-flesh union, and these future generations will spread out to care for and to rule over the earth. The work of Adam and Eve in the glorious garden God made marks the beginning of a long process by which their descendants are to develop the riches of creation. Adam and Eve's royal stewardship of Eden forms a microcosm of what God intends to happen to the whole creation as history unfolds.

Reflections for Today

The first few chapters of the Bible spotlight three great themes that will unfold as the story continues. First, the Maker; second, what God makes; and third, God's masterpiece—that's us!

The Maker

Though the word "unique" is almost a cliché in our advertising-saturated world, it's the only word that fits when it comes to the Creator in Genesis. There is only one God, and this God is unimaginably different from everything else there is. God is powerful, good, kind, wise, faithful, and holy. God is sovereign above all things. Yet the Creator bends to connect himself to everything else there is. And this Creator invites you and me into a relationship with himself. What a privilege it is to read God's story, realizing he is writing us into it!

What God Makes

The first chapters of Genesis picture a cosmos of exquisite beauty, harmony, joy, and pleasure. There is none of the pain, the evil, the death that are such normal elements of the world we know. But perhaps we should pause here to think about what we mean by that word "normal." It often means average, common, usual. In this sense, it may be "normal" to experience suffering and disappointment: "Stuff happens; that's just the way it is." But we can and do use the same word to describe not the way things are but the way things should be: for example, we say that a "normal" human temperature is 98.6° Fahrenheit or 36.8° Celsius.

It's in this latter sense of the word that Genesis offers an unforgettable snapshot of what a "normal" world looks like. Though you and I have never seen it just like this, we somehow know that this is the way our world was meant to be. The relationship sketched in Genesis between humankind and the rest of this remarkable world has often been misunderstood. Humankind is given the task to "rule" and "subdue" the earth—and to our shame we recognize that this has often been done in an oppressive and irresponsible way.

Just as we paid attention to what a "normal" creation was meant to look like, so we must see what it normally means to "rule" and "subdue" in the way God intended. It means to "develop and care for" the world God made good (Gen. 2:15). So, for example, careful stewards of God's creation might develop orchards and care for the trees so that they could eventually enjoy their fruit. This was the kind of developing and caring that God had in mind. But no obedient steward would carelessly pollute the land and make the trees unfruitful. Other stewards might tend trees and then cut them down for the sake of their wood. But no good steward would simply clear-cut those trees without caring for the continuing health of the forest and the other creatures that share it.

> **Genesis offers an unforgettable snapshot of what a "normal" world looks like. Though you and I have never seen it just like this, we somehow know that this is the way our world was meant to be.**

The same is true for all the other aspects of creation God gives us to be developed. Humans create culture in all its richness and diversity: marriage and friendship, art and scholarship, economic and political structures, games and sports, making things with our minds and hands, among a thousand other good gifts. God calls us as stewards to discover and to develop the potential built into creation, and to do so in a way that cares for and safeguards these good gifts, honors God as their Maker and Giver, and recognizes our own creaturely responsibility. And that brings us to the third spotlight: us!

The Masterpiece

If we were to hand you a photograph of, say, your graduating class from school, whose face would you seek out first? Right—your own! And so, of course, would we. We humans can be extraordinarily self-centered creatures! A reading of the early parts of Genesis may seem at first to flatter that kind of human vanity, since the fashioning of humankind, in all our male and female glory, is quite clearly the pinnacle of the Creator's work. But it should soon begin to sink in that the most glorious of all the qualities of the man and the woman who tend the garden is not their physical beauty, or their gifts of language and self-consciousness, or their intellect. Being made in the Creator's own image, our most glorious quality is that we reflect in miniature God's inexpressible glory. Of all God's creatures, only we can truly know what it means for God to love us, to speak to us, to listen to us—because only we have been made to do these things too. No other creature reflects God in this way.

God's image, stamped indelibly on our being, can never be fully eradicated. Yet the image of God in us has become horribly defaced by sin until it is sometimes hardly recognizable. No living human being fully reflects God's image in the way that Genesis suggests should be normal—except one. For that one, we must look ahead in the drama of Scripture to see God's image in humanity restored at last in Jesus. Paul calls Jesus the second Adam (Rom. 5:14; 1 Cor. 15:45). In Jesus we see the perfect image of God restored. By being like Jesus, we can become more and more what God the great Creator always intended us to be: living in fellowship with God, in harmony with the creation, fulfilled and happy in our calling to understand and enjoy and develop this good earth. Normal, at last.

Finding Our Place in the Story

1. We have seen that the first chapters of Genesis show a Creator who is intimately connected with the Creation. What are the dangers of losing sight of this, of thinking of God as vaguely "up there" in heaven?[4]

2. How do the Psalms (e.g. 8, 19, 33, 65, 104) show God as present and active in the world? How could this understanding help to reshape our view of the world?

3. The name Yahweh Elohim makes the point that the same God who redeems us is the one who created all things. Why is this so important? How do Christians sometimes separate salvation from creation, grace from material existence?

4. Why is it so important for Christians to remember that God made all things good (see Gen. 1:4, 12, 18, 21, 25, 31)? What does the apostle Paul mean when he says that to deny the goodness of creation is something "taught by demons" (1 Tim. 4:1-5)?

5. The Bible's account of Creation was written in part to argue against pagan myths. How does knowing this help us to understand and apply the first chapters of Genesis? What myths might the Creation story in Genesis battle against today?

6. What might be the relationship between the Genesis story and modern scientific ideas about the origins of the earth and of human life?

7. In Moses' time, only the Pharaoh was thought of as being in the image of a god. What does it mean for us that we are all made in God the Creator's own image?

8. Genesis shows the universe coming into being at a word from God, and in the New Testament that same Word is shown to give order to all things (see Heb. 1:3 and John 1:3). Why is this so important to the way we think about our world?

Act 2

Rebellion in the Kingdom—**Fall**

A driving feature of any story is its central conflict, the thing that goes wrong and needs to be fixed. Eugene Peterson describes the central conflict of the drama of Scripture in this way: "A catastrophe has occurred. We are no longer in continuity with our good beginning. We have been separated from it by a disaster. We are also, of course, separated from our good end. We are, in other words, in the middle of a mess."[1] Genesis 3 tells the tragic story of the entrance of sin into God's perfect world, often called (simply and ominously) the story of "the fall." This calamity threatens to mar the goodness of creation itself and to touch with evil every event that follows it. It is the cosmic conflict of the biblical story, the mess that still haunts our lives.

When discussing the story of the fall, some people too quickly resort to terms like "myth" and "legend." But this narrative is part of a larger structure (Gen. 2:4-3:24) introduced with the important phrase "This is the account of . . . ," suggesting that what follows really happened. Thus we need to take seriously the prehistorical reality of the events recorded in Genesis 3, even while recognizing that the details (including a talking serpent and symbolic trees) are unlike those of any historical text we are used to. In our view, the third chapter of Genesis reliably tells us about the mysterious origin of evil in God's world, rooted in the mutiny of the first human couple, though not as if it were a TV documentary.

> **Genesis reliably tells us about the mysterious origin of evil in God's world, rooted in the mutiny of the first human couple.**

The first two chapters of Genesis paint a picture of human beings created good and holy by God. Eden, their park-like home, is rich and fertile, a place of pleasure and delight. The LORD God himself spends time there with Adam and Eve (Gen. 3:8). Thus, at its beginning, the creation is redolent with *shalom*, the Old Testament word for peace that is meant to convey the rich, integrated, relational wholeness God intends for creation. Adam and Eve walk with God, they rejoice in each other, and the garden's fertile soil provides all they need as they tend its burgeoning plants. What could possibly go wrong?

We all know from our own experience the deep woundedness of our world, but what has caused it to be so? When we read about life in Eden, we long for our own lives to be like that. Why is our experience so different? Genesis 3 answers this question, though perhaps without all the details we would like to know. We are not told where the talking serpent comes from or who he is. (Only later in the Bible do we learn that this "creature" is also known as Satan; see Rev. 12:9.) How could such a creature disrupt God's good creation? These unanswered questions alert us to the impenetrable mystery that surrounds the origin of evil in the creation.

Part of being human is the freedom to choose. Even in God's good creation, Adam and Eve's freedom to love means that they may also choose not to love; hence they may experience temptation. But what would temptation involve for them? The answer is found in the mysterious "tree of the knowledge of good and evil" (Gen. 2:9). The serpent tempts them to eat from this tree, contrary to what God has told them to do (2:17; 3:1-5). But what does this mean?

Adam and Eve can obey God or they can defy God. They can yield to God's loving rule and enjoy life, or they can try to find their own way apart from God's instructions and experience death. As created beings, Adam and Eve are fully and wonderfully human as they live out their freedom under God's reign. The temptation they face through the serpent is to assert their autonomy: to become a law unto themselves rather than relying on God's word for direction.

The serpent subtly casts doubt on God's words to Adam and Eve, daring even to question God's own inherent goodness. The serpent suggests that God is afraid these human creatures might become equals once they know good and evil through eating the fruit of the tree. God has said that if they eat of it they will die, but the serpent suggests that to eat of it is to find the path to true life. In the light of these suggestions, the woman and the man see the tree as an opportunity for self-fulfillment. They take its fruit and eat.

At first, the serpent seems to have been telling the truth: Adam and Eve do not immediately die. Or do they? The physical life of Adam and Eve does not stop in the instant they taste the fruit: this isn't the poison apple of the fairy tale. But something deep inside them and between them does die. Their sense of themselves and their relationship with each other is shattered. They become self-conscious and try hurriedly to cover up their nakedness. Even worse, their relationship with the LORD God is also broken: they hide in fear and shame, cut off from God's life-giving presence.

God confronts Adam and Eve and declares judgment. God curses the serpent to crawl on the ground, the woman with pain in childbirth and oppression in her relationship with her husband, and even the ground itself, so that the man will toil and sweat in the struggle to till the hard, weedy soil. Finally God drives Adam and Eve out of Eden and bars them from the garden.

Even though the story does not explain the deep mystery of sin, it illumines much of sin's fundamental nature even in our lives today. It is a quest for autonomy, a desire to separate ourselves from God that always has tragic consequences. Just as Genesis 2 shows humankind in our created, unfallen relationships, so Genesis 3 focuses on the breakdown of those relationships following the human mutiny against the divine King. We humans are made for relationship, but sin drives us apart. Above all, we are made to enjoy relationship with God, but Adam and Eve's sin causes them to flee from him in fear, shame, and loneliness.

> **Even in this tragic tale of sin coming into the world, God refuses to give up on the creation and the kingdom.**

Is the story of the world to end so soon and so sadly? By no means. Even in this tragic tale of sin coming into the world, God refuses to give up on the creation and the kingdom. Though Adam and Eve flee, God graciously seeks them out. In declaring judgment, God curses the serpent and promises to put enmity between the serpent's offspring and that of the woman (Gen. 3:15). The woman's offspring will crush the serpent's head: God promises to extinguish the evil forces Adam and Eve have unleashed. This is the first biblical promise of the gospel: Christ will be "the seed of the woman" and will defeat Satan, though at great cost to himself in the "striking" of his "heel." In Genesis 3:21, God even provides for Adam and Eve's shame, clothing them with skins of animals. In the Old Testament, to remove someone's clothes could signify that they had lost their inheritance; by providing clothes for Adam and Eve, God shows that he has not given up on them. They still bear God's image in this world, and they will still "inherit the earth."

As Adam and Eve move east of Eden, their future seems bleak. Following their catastrophic disobedience, the wonderful garden now lies closed behind them while an uncertain and dangerous world looms ahead. How awful to face the LORD God when at last God found them! How hard to look God in the face! Still God's grace and promise shine through. God clothed them, taking away at least some of their shame and showing them continued care. And the mysterious promise about Eve's offspring who would one day crush the serpent's head still echoed in their heart.

Reflections for Today

What was so special about eating this forbidden fruit? In itself, it seems like a small thing. Yet here is where the story reaches forward into history to touch us and our lives and our world.

God created the man and the woman as stewards of God's good earth, made in God's own image. What a tremendous privilege for mere creatures to be as near to the Creator as that! And with the privilege comes a responsibility to bear that image obediently, acknowledging their limitations as creatures while trusting in the limitlessness of the Creator. The single rule God gives—to leave alone the fruit of one tree out of all the trees in the garden—is no trick. The Creator, who has put everything else under the rule of human stewards, leaves just one tangible reminder in their glorious world that he alone is the source and sustainer of all things, including their very lives. Their happiness in fulfilling their wonderful task as God's stewards and companions, their joy in the beauties of the garden, and their delight in each other's company all depend on that single truth.

But the serpent twists this truth, making it seem that God is selfishly holding back some good thing from these human creatures. And they choose to believe the serpent. Though we often trivialize sin, this story should make us pay attention to what it really is. Sin is not a mere mistake, nor the inevitable

> In rejecting the way of the Creator we reach for a bigger slice of life and find out that it tastes like death.

result of being human and limited. Sin is a decision to choose our own way instead of the way God has built into creation. It is to become our own rule-makers instead of responding to the divine Ruler in obedience.

As limited, human creatures, Adam and Eve were bound to follow some rule, for that is the way God made them. The serpent didn't give them ultimate freedom; just a different authority to obey. They fell for it, as we all do.

In rejecting the way of the Creator we reach for a bigger slice of life and find out that it tastes like death. We reach out for what we think will be more than God gives but end up with far less: broken friendships, marriages, and families; corrupt governments and legal institutions; starvation in many parts of the world and a plague of obesity elsewhere; the oppression of the weak by the strong, of one race or one gender by another. Sadly, we have come to see all of this as normal.

Sin is not normal—it's not a reflection of what God originally intended for us and our world. We can think of sin in various ways.

Sin is rebellion. It's treason of the creature (that's us) against our Creator. We have withdrawn our allegiance from a loving, good, and wise Father and given it to a lying snake.

Sin is idolatry. We were made to serve Someone or Something: it is part of the very fabric of our being. We can choose not to serve and obey God, but that doesn't mean we can choose not to serve at all! Adam and Eve shut out God's word only to open their ears to Satan. When we choose not to serve God, we inevitably find another center for our lives. We can see this in human societies that have tried to serve the gods of reason, science, or technology and in the lives of individual men and women who have tried to make a god of pleasure, fame, money, or even a relationship. Such gods can never deliver what they promise.

Sin is an attempt to achieve autonomy, to decide for ourselves what is good, right, true, and worthwhile. While trying to establish our own standards and looking for freedom outside of God's good order and purpose, we become trapped in our own devices. Ever since that first human rebellion, sin's destructive, life-negating power has tainted human lives and cultures.

But sin cannot (usually) destroy the goodness of creation outright. Rather, it twists and distorts it. So, for example, sin doesn't destroy sexuality but perverts it, turning it toward adultery and other exploitative relationships. Sin doesn't destroy the state but twists it away from public justice. Sin doesn't destroy human reason but turns it toward evil or selfish ends. We cannot blame any part of the good creation for the mess we are in. Government, the economy, schools, authority, technology—all of these are part of a creation order that was made good. But all have become twisted, corrupted, polluted, and distorted by human rebellion against the Creator.

That's the bad news. But here's the good news: God will not leave the world this way! God promises to restore it to what it was meant to be. Those who follow Jesus now are called to point the way to the cosmic restoration yet to come.

Finding Our Place in the Story

1. We often think of sin as something trivial, as if it were merely breaking one of God's rules in the way that some of us break the speed limit on the highways. How do these concepts (from the discussion of Genesis 3) add to our view of what sin is?

   - *Who am I?* What does it mean to be human?
   - *Where am I?* Where did our world come from?
   - *What is wrong?* Why does this world seem to be so troubled?
   - *What is the remedy?* Can humans alone fix the problems of the world?

2. Sin has marred our relationships with God, with each other, and with the creation. Discuss concrete ways in which each of these relationships has been twisted out of shape by sin.

3. We have seen that sin does not ordinarily destroy what God has made, but it does distort it. Discuss some ways in which God's good gifts (such as food, drink, sexuality, family, work, and leisure) have been distorted by sin.

4. Consider this statement: "Our world is not 'normal' and will not become so until Jesus finishes his work of restoration." What is "normal" in any case?

Act 3

The King Chooses Israel—Redemption Initiated

Scene 1: A People for the King

Genesis: The Origins of Israel

Sin Unleashed and God's Response

When Adam and Eve were banished from their home in Eden, they did not cease to be what God had created. The effect of the fall on all of us is not that we stop being human—we remain in the image of God (Gen. 5:1; 9:6). But our rebellion has deeply affected how we are human. Thus Adam and Eve remain married even after their sin, and Eve gives birth to two healthy sons. These four are a family, as God had planned for them before the fall. But as the story continues in Genesis 4, the terrible change within the human heart becomes apparent.

Cain and Abel are the first brothers. Cain is a farmer, Abel a shepherd. Instead of enjoying companionship and supporting each other in their different jobs, Cain burns with jealousy toward Abel. It comes to a head when each of the brothers makes an offering to God. Abel's is accepted, but Cain's is rejected, evidently because of the evil inside him. Cain's resentment festers. He invites Abel to go for a walk in one of his fields, and there Cain murders his brother. The unthinkable has happened. The family that God meant to be a source of companionship and joy has become a place of jealousy, rage, and murder.

In response to the horror of this murder, we might expect God to destroy everything immediately. But the good order that God has established for his creation remains. Cain marries and has a son named Enoch; he and his family are still humans in the image of God. But the story demonstrates clearly that humans now have a terrible propensity to wreak havoc on themselves and others. Family life and other good gifts can be sources of pain and vengeance.

It's against this background that we need to understand the events that follow: Cain builds a city, and people begin to develop culture in many different directions (4:17-22).

"Culture" is the name we give to organized activities within society, such as making music or building houses or founding economic or political structures. In Genesis 4 we read about Cain (who built a city called Enoch), Jabal (the ancestor of those who live in tents and keep livestock), Jubal (the ancestor of those who play the lyre and pipe), Tubal-Cain (who made all kinds of bronze and iron tools), and Lamech (who wrote poetry). We must not assume that all this cultural activity is a result of sin. On the contrary, these cultural achievements come about when men and women develop the potential God has built into creation. Such pursuits are essentially good, not evil. As we saw in the first act of the story, cultural activity is a fundamental way in which we may serve and glorify God. In the context of Genesis 4, however, we are reminded that sinful humans misdirect such good, cultural activities.

> **Cultural activity is a fundamental way in which we may serve and glorify God.**

Knowing what we do about Cain, our hearts sink as we think of him building and controlling a city, even though building a city is one important part of developing the potential hidden in creation. It's wrong to think that God's goal for creation stops at being only a pristine, rural park. God intends for cities to be developed as well. But the fact that Cain is the one who develops the first city makes us wary of the possible corruption of God's intention. As we know too well, cities can become places of squalor and oppression as well as places where human culture flourishes. How will Cain's jealousy and rage affect life in and around the city he calls Enoch, after his son? The cultural development of the city—in itself, potentially a good outworking of humankind's mandate to develop the creation—begins with a man who has already shown his contempt for God's supreme rule.

Poetry is a wonderful gift from God, and the Bible contains many songs and poems that develop the beauty and power of language in obedience to God's order. Lamech is the first poet in the Bible. But in his poem, God's wonderful gift has already been twisted into an instrument to threaten with revenge and violence: "If Cain is avenged seven times, then Lamech seventy-seven times" (Gen. 4:24). Lamech subverts the gift of poetic language in a way that ignores or denies God's rule for the creation and God's role as the Giver.

Through a genealogy, the fifth chapter of Genesis tells the story of the human race from Adam to Noah, Lamech's son. Noah means "rest," and Lamech's great hope is that through Noah's birth, God will grant rest to humans from the difficulties of work in the fallen creation (5:28-29). But things do not get better for the creation—at least not at first.

Genesis 6:1-8 tells the story of how evil reaches a climax among humankind, and God decides to destroy the world through a great flood and begin anew. Noah will be like a new Adam. He will bring a new possibility of rest as Lamech hoped—but only after terrible judgment. The flood God will send upon the earth is to be catastrophic and universal, a sort of "uncreation." Huge amounts of water inundate everything as "the springs of the great deep burst forth," and it rains steadily for forty days (7:11-12).

But though the judgment against sin will be terrible, still God tenaciously keeps his gracious commitment to the creation. God tells Noah what will happen and instructs him to build an ark in which Noah, his extended family, and two of each kind of animal on earth will be delivered from the flood. People *and* animals. Why take these smelly animals into the ark? Because God's salvation does not stop with humankind: it embraces the whole creation—including the animals (Rom. 8:21). Human sin spreads brokenness and destruction to the whole creation, including plants and animals, but God's salvation will restore peace and wholeness to all living things. If we ignore this emphasis in Scripture our view of salvation is too narrow.

> **God's salvation does not stop with humankind: it embraces the whole creation.**

The story of the flood reveals a God who is both holy Judge and gracious Redeemer. When Noah and his family finally emerge from the ark with the animals, God makes a solemn covenant with Noah and his family (Gen. 9:8-17). "Covenant," the word that describes the relationship between God and people, is helpfully defined by O. Palmer Robertson as a "bond in blood sovereignly administered."[1] Consider the three main elements in this definition:

- *A bond.* The covenant speaks of a deeply personal relationship between God and people, a relationship so close that God binds or ties himself to them, and them to him. In later covenants with Israel, a favorite expression is, "I will be your God and you will be my people" (as in Jer. 7:23).
- *In blood.* A covenant is a serious, legally established relationship, like a marriage (also described as a covenant in the Old Testament). The serious, public nature of a covenant is symbolized in rituals involving sacrifice and the shedding of blood (as in Gen. 8:20-22).
- *Sovereignly administered.* This covenant is not a relationship between equal partners who hammer out mutually agreeable terms. As the sovereign Lord, God alone can establish the terms of the covenant relationship and ultimately keep them.

When God tells Noah that he will "establish his covenant" with him (Gen. 6:18), this word "covenant" refers to an existing relationship, not to something brand new. In Genesis 9, God renews the original creation covenant through Noah. We see this by the way in which Genesis 9 depicts Noah as a second Adam. God commissions Noah in the same way Adam was—and in virtually the same words. God says, "Be fruitful and multiply, and fill the earth" (cf. 1:28; 9:1, 7, NRSV). Though God is making a new start with Noah, his purposes for his creation remain what they always were. And the content of God's covenant with Noah extends to the whole of creation. In Genesis 8:21 God

> God acts in and through Noah to fulfill what God had always intended for the whole of creation.

promises never again to curse the ground or destroy every living creature. And in Genesis 9:8-17 we read that God's covenant is with Noah and his descendants and with every living creature. The rainbow is a sign of this gracious covenant established between God and "all life on the earth" (9:17).

Through this covenant God enters a special relationship with Noah and his family, but its foundation is God's continuing covenant with the creation. God acts in and through Noah to fulfill what God always intended for all creation.

But alas, God's new start does not usher in the fullness of rest that Noah's father Lamech had hoped for. The earth is peopled again from Noah's three sons (9:18), but sin's destructive force soon shows up again (9:20-28). Once more, cultural development is ambivalent. On the one hand, agriculture advances: Noah is the first to plant a vine and to develop the wonderful art of making wine (9:20). But while wine itself and the craft of making it are good gifts in themselves, they can also be misused. The world's first vintner becomes drunk and disgraces himself and his family, lying openly naked in his tent to sleep it off, where his son Ham discovers him. It is hard to be sure what the problem is in Ham's response to Noah's behavior: is there a sexual offence involved, or is Ham's gossip about his father's nakedness an act of sinful disrespect? Either way, there is further family breakdown. Noah curses Canaan, the son of Ham (thus cursing the people who will descend in this line of his own family) and blesses Shem (from whose line the Israelites will descend).

Genesis 10 tells of the world's nations emerging from the sons of Noah. This is a positive fulfillment of God's command to Adam, which is then repeated to Noah: "Be fruitful and multiply, and fill the earth." However, at this stage in the story, no matter how positive the cultural and numerical growth, we've come to expect the fallout of sin.

The next chapter of Genesis tells the story of the tower of Babel, a monumental, communal attempt by Adam's race to wrest human autonomy from God once more. As we've already noted, the impulse to build a city is part of normal cultural development within God's world. But this impulse can be misdirected, and in the story of Babel that happens on a massive scale. As people migrate eastward, they build a city with a huge tower. This is their way of asserting their own will against God's desire that humans should be spread and scattered throughout the world ("fill the earth").

Babel stands as a monument to the perennial human desire to build our own kingdom apart from God, to "make a name for ourselves, and not be scattered over the face of the whole earth" (11:4). But God brings an abrupt halt to the prideful building program in way that can only bring a smile to the reader. The builders can't understand each other as a cacophony of different languages breaks out among them. In frustration, the people scatter, effectively putting an end to their ambitious, idolatrous building program.

Though Genesis 11 marks a high point in human pride and sinfulness, God once again tempers judgment with mercy. The very next scene of the biblical drama shows yet another new beginning for humankind as God steadfastly pursues his purpose for his creation.

The Abrahamic Covenant: Blessed to Be a Blessing

Thus far, the biblical story has focused on the lives and acts of the whole of humankind. But now, in response to the catastrophe of Babel, God takes the initiative once more and turns to one clan and then one man, Abraham. Indeed, Abraham and his descendants are the major concern of the rest of Genesis.

Toward the end of Genesis 11, the story narrows to the descendants of Noah's son Shem, and then to the little clan of Terah in Haran (in what is now northern Iraq). And then all the attention falls on one man, Abraham. God calls Abraham to leave his country, his people, and his father's house to go to the land that God will show him (12:1-3). With this radical call God invites Abraham to leave his home and wander to an unknown place. God accompanies this call (as we'll see in a moment) with a staggering promise. Wonderfully, Abraham does give up all for the sake of God's call. Abraham follows where God will lead and sets out with his wife, Sarah, his nephew Lot, and their extended family.

What is God up to in all of this? By narrowing the focus to Abraham, has God given up on all other peoples? The biblical answer is a resounding no! The first three verses of Genesis 12 spell out for Abraham the blessing God will extend to the whole world through him. God promises

- to make Abraham's family into a great nation;
- to bless him;
- to make his name great;
- to make him a blessing;
- to bless those who bless him and curse (or judge) those who judge him; and
- to bless all peoples on earth through Abraham!

Here the story begins to reveal how God will respond to what has gone wrong in his creation. Through Abraham God will bring into being a nation, Israel, to be God's own people among all the other peoples of the world. Through this nation God will bring blessing to all the other peoples of the earth (18:18-19). Far from giving up on the world and its people, God digs his commitment into the soul of one man and the soil of one place.

Though much of the biblical story from here on focuses on Abraham and his descendants, God never forgets that through one person, many people and nations will know God's blessing. A closer look at the careful way the story is told reveals God's strategy. The word "bless" is repeated five times in the two verses that contain God's blessing to Abraham. This stands in bold opposition to the five-fold occurrence of the word "curse" in chapters 1-11. God's curse or judgment on humankind has meant their loss of freedom (3:14-16), their alienation from the soil (3:17-19), their estrangement from one another (4:11), and their moral and spiritual degradation (9:25). The repetition of "bless" in 12:2-3 declares that through Abraham, God is working to reverse the effect of the curse on creation. Though sin has brought God's curse on creation, God will reverse it with blessing. As we sing of Christ in Isaac Watts's beloved Christmas carol, "He comes to make his blessings flow far as the curse is found." God calls Abraham to be the human channel through whom divine restoration will flow over the whole world.

> God calls Abraham to be the human channel through whom divine restoration will flow over the whole world.

Through Abraham, "all peoples on earth will be blessed." This final climactic clause points to the ultimate result of God's choosing Abraham. God narrows the redemptive focus to one man, one nation. But God's ultimate purpose extends with redemptive blessing to the whole creation. From the beginning, God's people are to be "missionary," chosen to be a channel of blessing to others.

God's relationship with Abraham is described as a covenant in Genesis 15 and 17, like his relationship with Noah earlier in the story. In chapter 15, God promises Abraham—who has not yet fathered even one child!—that his descendants will one day be as numerous as the stars of the sky. God also promises to give Abraham's descendants the land of Canaan. When Abraham questions God's promise, God initiates a covenant ceremony. Abraham halves three animals and arranges them so that there is an aisle between the halves. God passes through the animals in the form of a smoking fire pot. In this covenant ceremony, mysterious to us but well known to the people of the day, God signifies that if he does not keep his promise, he will be torn limb from limb like these animals (cf. Jer. 34:18-20). This is the Lord's solemn promise to Abraham, the guarantee of the covenant between them.

Some time later God appears again to Abraham, who is by now ninety-nine years old and still childless. Abraham falls face down before God, and God confirms the covenant, promising Abraham numerous descendants (17:4-6) and a land and home for his people (17:8). Furthermore, God will be the great King of the nation that will descend from Abraham (17:7). In Genesis 17:10 God introduces the mark of circumcision for all males belonging to Abraham's line. In the ancient Near East, circumcision was practised by most of the nations. Here God radically transforms this common cultural practice for his people. For the Israelites, it becomes a sign cut into their flesh of the covenant between God and Abraham and his descendants.

God's covenant with Abraham contains three elements: a personal relationship with God, the growth of his family into a nation, and land for this nation's home. These promises to one man are always made by God with a view to blessing all nations through him. The rest of the story in the Pentateuch (the five "books of Moses," Genesis through Deuteronomy) describes the partial fulfillment of these promises and the formation of God's people.

God also tells Abraham that he will not see his descendants inherit the promised land (Gen. 15:15). Yet he has to learn to trust God against all the odds. "Abraham believed the LORD, and he credited it to him as righteousness" (15:6). This key text reappears as the story continues (Gal. 3:6; Rom. 4:3), showing that faith in God's promises is the key element of God's work in our lives and in the world.

> Faith in God's promises is the key element of God's work in our lives and in the world.

The stories of Abraham and Sarah reveal how difficult it is to maintain such trust, particularly as the years roll on and Sarah is still not pregnant. At one point Abraham has had enough of these promises. He laughs at the ludicrous idea of this old man and woman with a child (17:17), and Sarah joins him in laughter (18:12). Abraham tries to find a way of fulfilling the promise through his own effort, fathering a child by his servant Hagar with disastrous family consequences. Eventually, however, God does bless Sarah with the child of promise. By this time, Abraham is already a hundred years old (21:5).

But the testing of Abraham's faith in God's promises isn't over yet. In Genesis 22, God tells Abraham to take his "only son Isaac" and sacrifice him on Mount Moriah. After all those years of waiting for a son, Abraham is to take Isaac and kill him. So great is Abraham's faith that he prepares to obey. At the very last moment, God's messenger stays Abraham's hand, poised in midair with a knife to kill his son. God provides a ram to die in Isaac's place, and Abraham makes another sacrifice. With that test, God strongly reaffirms the covenant promise: "Through your offspring all nations on earth will be blessed, because you have obeyed me" (22:18).

Chapters 25 to 36 of Genesis narrate the stories of Isaac and his sons Esau and Jacob. From Jacob's sons come the twelve tribes of Israel. Although God's purpose in calling Abraham was to bring blessing to the whole world, for the time being the biblical story continues to focus on the family line through whom this blessing will come: the twelve sons of Jacob, whose families are to become the twelve tribes of the nation of Israel.

Three themes bind these stories together. First, God reaffirms the promises he gave to Abraham to his son and grandson, so that God now calls himself "the God of Abraham, the God of Isaac and Jacob" (Ex. 3:6). To Isaac (Gen. 26:3-5) and Jacob (28:13-15) God promises to make them a great nation, to give them the land, and ultimately to bless all nations through them.

Second, these stories honestly confront the sinful character of those whom God chooses. A repeated theme in these stories, especially those about Jacob and Joseph, is the bitter breakdown in family relationships. The feuding between Jacob and Esau and the jealousy of Joseph's brothers serve as stark reminders that broken human relationships began with the sin of Adam and Eve; not even God's chosen people are immune from the effects of sin. God will work through such people to bring blessing to the world, but first God has to work in them and with them to bring reconciliation and maturity.

The third theme common to these narratives is that God overcomes many obstacles to work out a plan for the chosen people. The patriarchs' wives are barren or are taken into other men's harems. Natural disasters such as famine threaten to overtake God's people. Time and again the stupidity and sinfulness of the patriarchs themselves puts them and their families—and God's purposes—in peril. And yet, through all of this human turmoil, God remains faithful to the promise to Abraham.

This pervasive theme of God's constant faithfulness is probably related to one of the names for God in these stories of the patriarchs: *El Shaddai* (17:1; 28:3; 35:11; 48:3; "God Almighty" in many English versions). In Exodus 6:3 God tells Moses that he has revealed himself to Abraham, Isaac, and Jacob by this name, the precise meaning of which is unclear. *El Shaddai* seems to evoke the idea that God has the power to overcome all barriers and work through all circumstances to keep promises. This theme of God's providence emerges with particular clarity in the Joseph story (Gen. 37-50). In Genesis 45:5-7, Joseph recognizes that all that has happened to him has been ordained by God to "preserve for [his father's family] a remnant on earth and to save [their] lives by a great deliverance" (cf. 50:20).

By the end of the Genesis story, God's promise to Abraham that he would have many descendants has been partially fulfilled (47:27; Ex. 1:6-7). Jacob's children have become a large, flourishing group in Egypt. Old Jacob gathers his whole family around to offer a parting blessing and a dim but surprising look into the future (49:1-28). When he comes to his son Judah, Jacob's inspired words echo mysteriously down the ages. "You are a lion's cub, Judah. . . . The scepter will not depart from Judah nor the ruler's staff from between his feet, until he to whom it belongs shall come and the obedience of the nations be his" (49:9-10; see also Rev. 5:5). Here again, as the story pauses before the next scene, we hear a hint of God's ultimate saving purpose.

Exodus: Formation of a People
God Forms Israel by a Mighty Act of Redemption
As the biblical story resumes in Exodus, four hundred years after Abraham, his descendants remain in Egypt. Joseph and his brothers have died but their descendants have multiplied as God had promised they would. But what of God's other promises to Abraham—to provide a relationship with him and to

give his people a land of their own? As the Exodus narrative begins, these promises still seem a long way off.

A new pharaoh "to whom Joseph meant nothing" has come on the scene. Because this Egyptian ruler fears the growing strength of the Israelite nation within his country, he subjects them to brutal slave labor and even orders the killing of all newborn males among them in an effort to keep the population of the Israelites in check. Paradoxically, this oppression becomes the impetus for the Israelites' liberation from Egypt. When they cry out to God in their suffering and oppression, "God hear[s] their groaning and he remember[s] his covenant with Abraham, with Isaac and with Jacob" (Ex. 2:24).

Again, the scope of God's purpose narrows to one family. A boy named Moses is born to a Hebrew family. Lest he be slaughtered like the other baby boys born to the Israelites, Moses' mother puts him in a basket and places it among reeds at the edge of the Nile River. Pharaoh's daughter, who has come to bathe in the river, finds the baby and adopts him as her own child. Without God's name being mentioned at all, the story recognizes his hidden hand as Moses receives the best education Egypt can offer in the heart of Pharaoh's own household!

As a young man, Moses sympathizes with the suffering of his people. On one occasion he observes an Israelite being beaten by an Egyptian. Enraged, Moses kills the Egyptian and then has to flee because there was a witness to what he had done. Though Pharaoh tries to have Moses killed, Moses escapes to Midian and becomes a shepherd (2:11-17).

While caring for the flocks of his father-in-law near Mount Horeb, Moses has an astonishing encounter—God speaks to him from a burning bush (Ex. 3). Though the bush burns, it is miraculously not consumed by the flames. God tells Moses to take off his sandals, as the ground Moses is standing on is holy, and identifies himself to Moses as the God of Abraham, Isaac, and Jacob. God tells Moses that he has heard the cry of his oppressed people and will send Moses back to Pharaoh to bring his people out of Egypt into the land he has promised them. Moses responds reluctantly, wondering how he can convince the Israelites that it is really God who has sent him. God replies, "I AM WHO I AM. This is what you are to say to the Israelites: 'I AM has sent me to you'" (3:14).

This episode introduces us to the most common and distinctive name for God in the Old Testament: *Yahweh*, generally translated in English versions of the Bible as "Lord." (The Jews consider it blasphemous to take the very name of God on their lips, so they substitute *Adonai* or Lord, indicated in most translations with all capital letters.) The name *Yahweh* occurs some 6,800 times in the Old Testament, and much has been written about its precise meaning. Numerous translations and suggestions have been made about this name and about the phrase it comes from (in 3:14). Perhaps the best translation of this expression is "I will be who I am." Understood this way, the name *Yahweh* indicates not just that God is present now, but that he will be

> God demonstrates faithfulness to the promises made to Abraham by rescuing the nation descended from Abraham, taking them out of slavery, and placing them in the promised land.

faithfully God for [his people] in the history that is to follow. . . . Israel need not be concerned about divine arbitrariness or capriciousness. God can be counted on to be who God is. Israel understands its history from this name and this name from its history. The name will shape Israel's story, but the story will also give greater texture to the name.[2]

God demonstrates faithfulness to the promises made to Abraham by rescuing the nation descended from Abraham, taking them out of slavery, and placing them in the promised land. In God's call to Moses (6:6-7), the name *Yahweh* is particularly associated with this marvelous act of deliverance from Egypt:

Therefore, say to the Israelites: "I am the Lord, and I will bring you out from under the yoke of the Egyptians. I will free you from being slaves to them, and I will redeem you with an outstretched arm and with mighty acts of judgment. I will take you as my own people, and I will be your God. Then you will know that I am the Lord your God, who brought you out from under the yoke of the Egyptians."

The big obstacle to the Israelites' leaving Egypt is Pharaoh, who regards his own power as absolute. When Moses and Aaron ask Egypt's king to let the Israelites go so that they can hold a festival to the Lord in the desert, Pharaoh replies, "Who is the Lord, that I should obey him and let Israel go? I do not know the Lord and I will not let Israel go" (5:2). Thus "Pharaoh and [Yahweh] face off. Both claim Israel. Both demand Israel's service and allegiance for themselves . . . [but] the course of the plagues makes it evident who really possesses supreme power."[3]

God sends Moses (and Aaron, Moses' spokesman) to confront Pharaoh, who "hardens his heart" and refuses to acknowledge the Lord or to let the Israelites go. Through a series of ten plagues, Pharaoh is confronted with God's authority and power. The first nine are blood in the Nile, frogs, gnats, flies, diseased livestock, boils, hail and thunder, locusts, and dense darkness. Finally a deadly disease descends on the firstborn males in the whole of Egypt, both human and animal. But the firstborn of the Israelites are spared.

To understand the plagues we need to recognize that God is at work in these amazing events, showing Pharaoh and the Egyptians God's sovereign power over the whole creation. The plagues seem to be directed against various Egyptian gods, as Exodus 12:12 suggests—"I will bring judgment on all the gods of Egypt"—though it's difficult to relate each plague to any one god in particular. God's confrontation with Pharaoh and the Egyptian gods demonstrates *Yahweh*'s power, so that his "name might be proclaimed in all the earth" (9:16).

Defeated at last, Pharaoh gives in and lets the Israelites go. Exodus 12 shows how this great deliverance becomes the basis for the annual Feast of the Passover, in which Israel is to remember God's mighty act of deliverance. The term "Passover" comes from the final plague, in which God destroys the Egyptians' firstborn male children and animals but "passes over" the Israelites. In years to come, this deliverance from oppression and slavery profoundly shapes the memory of the Israelites. They are a free people only because God is their mighty Liberator.

Pharaoh does make one last desperate attempt to restrain the Israelites, sending his armies after them as they flee Egypt. But the sea, that great symbol of power and chaos (which is also under the Lord's control), overwhelms Pharaoh's armies (Ex. 14). Exodus 15 records the victory song of Moses and the Israelites, in which God is pictured as a mighty warrior who has won the battle for his people and will reign forever. The hymn expresses confidence that God will continue to direct the newly redeemed people and give them the land promised to their forefathers. When God eventually plants the Israelites in the land, it will be a major step toward the recovery and restoration of the whole creation.

Israel Is Bound to God in Covenant

Three months after leaving Egypt under Moses' leadership, the Israelites arrive at Mount Sinai, the same area where Moses first met God. But there is a difference: then, God spoke to one man from a burning bush; now, the whole mountain is ablaze as God meets with the redeemed people (19:16). God now calls not just an individual but an entire nation. God is revealed to the Israelites in thunder and lightning on the mountain in an awesome reminder of God's character and power. This too is holy ground.

At the mountain the Israelites are reminded through Moses both what God has done for them in the past and what God's purpose is for their future (19:3-6). God has brought them out of Egypt like an eagle carrying its exhausted young on its wings. The formation of Israel as God's people is utterly dependent on God's gracious acts on their behalf: "I . . . brought you to myself" (19:4). The Lord's intention is to have a relationship with people.

But why has God chosen them? God's intent is revealed in Exodus 19:5-6. God has called Israel for a special purpose. Out of all nations, they are elected to be God's own treasured possession! But as we noted with Abraham, election is not just Israel's privilege: it is also a call to service for the sake of all the other nations. If Israel lives under God's reign, they will be a "kingdom of priests" and a "holy nation," witnessing to the rule of God over creation by their very lives.

Holiness is one of the most important attributes the Bible ascribes to God. It tells us that God is special, different from all creation, and full of goodness. Israel is called by God to be holy as God is holy, to be different, a royal priesthood among the nations. Just as the priests of Israel mediate between God and the people, Israel is called to mediate between the Lord and all the nations. God intends for Israel to be "a display-people, a showcase to the world of how being in covenant with Yahweh changes a people."[4] As the Israelites obey God, they will demonstrate what life under God's reign looks like. The nations will then catch

> **Holiness tells us that God is special, different from all creation, and full of goodness.**

a glimpse of God's plan for all people. The whole of Israel's experience, including family life, law, politics, economics, and recreation, will reflect God's character and God's original created intention for human life. Israel's life under God is to testify to the living presence of God with his people. It is to be such a full and rich human life that the nations of the earth will be drawn to it. In this way Israel will fulfill God's covenant with Abraham to bless all the nations.

God's rescue of the Israelites comes about not because they deserve to be rescued or have earned it in any way by their obedience to God, but because of God's gracious love for them (Deut. 7:7-8).

But Israel will achieve their destiny to become a royal priesthood and holy nation only if they choose a life of active obedience under God's reign. The rest of the Old Testament is the story of how faithful or unfaithful Israel is to this call: "The history of Israel from this point on is in reality merely a commentary upon the degree of fidelity with which Israel adhered to this Sinai-given vocation."[5]

Israel hears God's call in the context of a covenant. In Exodus 19-24 a covenant relationship is established between God and the Israelites at Mount Sinai. Scholars have long noted the similarities between ancient Near Eastern vassal treaties and this Sinai covenant. A vassal treaty was a contract established between a great conquering king and a nation coming under his control. Around the time of Moses, this was the means by which the Hittite kings administered their empire. The shape of the covenant in Exodus is much like one of these vassal treaties. It is clearly not a treaty between equals: God is the great King, and Israel the subordinate nation. In this case Israel has come under God's control and become God's people not because they have been conquered (as the Hittite kings would conquer neighboring tribes), but because God has liberated them from slavery in Egypt.

These Scriptures imply that God is a great King, something like the powerful Hittite conquerors and yet incomparably greater. This image of God's status gives us important insight into how the Israelite nation becomes God's own people. Just as a conquering king takes seriously every aspect of the life of a nation that is to become his vassal state, so the liberating God intends to rule over every aspect of the life of Israel.

We see this clearly in the instructions he gives to regulate and shape every aspect of the Israelites' lives. We generally call these instructions "law." Such law is not entirely new to the Israelites; they have had ample experience of law during their time as enslaved people in Egypt. The law God gives to Moses for the Israelites bears all the marks of ancient Near Eastern law. God is not calling people to live in an eccentric, unhistorical fashion: they are to be people of their own historical time and place. And yet the law is recast with some distinctive elements to reflect God's own character and to achieve what God desires for creation. For example, although the law of that time valued property above people and made the punishment for stealing greater than that for murder, Israel's law values people above mere property; for only people, of all God's creatures, have been fashioned in his image.

> The Ten Commandments, or "Ten Words," are the core principles that are to shape God's people so that their lives will reflect God's character.

The Ten Commandments, or "Ten Words," (Ex. 20; Deut. 5) are the core principles that are to shape God's people so that their lives will reflect God's character. The detailed instructions that follow the Ten Words apply these general principles to every aspect of Israel's life before God (Ex. 20-22). Only as God's law shapes their whole lives will Israel truly be a royal priesthood and a holy nation, fulfilling their calling to become a channel of God's blessing to all other nations.

Though each of the Ten Commandments (except the fourth and fifth) is expressed in a negative form, all have positive implications. The first commandment not only prohibits the inclusion of any other "gods" in Israel's formal worship, but also positively directs Israel to serve the Lord alone. The second commandment, forbidding the people to make any image of the Lord or any other god, is unique for Israel's time and place. Alone among the nations of the ancient Near East, only Israel is to have no physical image of their deity—no picture or sculpture—as an object of worship. This command alone would have astonished Israel's neighbors and raised profound questions about the nature of Israel's God. In that time, having no image in one's sanctuary would be taken to mean that one believed in no god at all! The Israelites must realize and witness to the fact that theirs is no ordinary "god," but the very Lord of heaven and earth.

Similarly, though God has revealed himself to Israel as *Yahweh*, God forbids them to use that name in an attempt to exercise magical power. The third commandment teaches that the Lord is to be respected, and the people must make no attempt to manipulate God's name for their own purposes. The fourth commandment commends work as worthy and necessary—"Six days you shall labor"—but it also firmly places work within the context of the people's relationship to God. The Sabbath day of rest establishes the reality that God's people live by God's grace and not by their own labors.

The fifth to tenth commandments regulate relationships among God's people as new generations are inducted into life among God's people in healthy social structures. The fifth commandment insists on parental authority and responsibility. In the remaining "Words" God forbids murder, adultery, stealing, false testimony, and coveting among his chosen people. These laws call Israel to be a community in which the divine shalom of peace and harmony characterizes life within the family and among neighbors.

The Ten Commandments are good news. They tell Israel how to live in a way that pleases God, is best for themselves, and displays God's purposes for humanity to the nations. As Creator, the Lord's instructions fit with the way he has made the world and its people. So the commandments are keys to living fully human lives, not constraints to make life difficult.

In Exodus 20:22-23:33 many detailed stipulations follow from the general commands. These deal with a variety of subjects such as worship, slavery, assault, kidnapping, sexual offenses, economic activities, religious festivals, and the care of animals, among many others. All of life comes within the scope of the Lord's reign. As we consider the meaning of these laws, it's important to remember that they were given to the Israelites living in the ancient Near East. The commandments remain profoundly relevant for our lives before God, but we cannot necessarily apply them in the same ways as the ancient nation of Israel was to observe them. For example, in Israelite society the penalties for breaking many of the commandments were very severe, so that, for instance, anyone who worshiped another god was to be put to death. Though we should continue to learn from this that God takes the sin of idolatry extremely seriously, we also recognize that this is no longer God's intent under the new covenant.

In Exodus 24 the Israelites ratify the stipulations of the covenant with a ritual ceremony in which they commit to obey. Moses recites the laws that the Israelites are agreeing to and then writes them down. Next he builds an altar and sets up twelve pillars that stand for the twelve tribes of Israel. This covenant is with the whole people of God and, like the pillars, is to be permanent. Finally, Moses dashes half of the blood from the sacrifices against the altar and sprinkles half on the people themselves. All this blood indicates that sacrifice is necessary for sinners to come into God's presence. The blood is called the "blood of the covenant," a phrase that Jesus will use at the Last Supper. The blood also signifies the seriousness of the relationship: it is a way of saying, "May this happen to us, may our own blood be poured out, if we fail to keep the terms of the agreement."

As the ratification ceremony ends, the seventy elders—along with Moses and Aaron, Nadab and Abihu—go up the mountain. There the communion between God and people, so central to the covenant, is wonderfully enacted: the elders "see" God, and they eat and drink together with him (24:9-11). God has promised a relationship with people; here that promise is well on its way to being fulfilled. God comes to dwell with people.

God intends to become a permanent part of the life of Israel. He instructs Moses to gather from among the Israelites the materials required to build a complex tent structure, the tabernacle, and then gives detailed instructions for its construction. The formal worship life of Israel will take place here. The priests and Levites will preside over the sacrifices and offerings of the Israelites, but the main point of the tabernacle is that it is a portable sanctuary, God's personal residence among the covenant people. "Then I will dwell among the Israelites and be their God. They will know that I am the LORD their God, who brought them out of Egypt so that I might dwell among them. I am the LORD their God" (29:45-46).

The main point of the tabernacle is that it is a portable sanctuary, God's personal residence among the covenant people.

Nearly a third of Exodus details the plans for the tabernacle, and these details are repeated as it is actually being built. The sheer length and complexity of these instructions makes an important point: such a residence cannot be taken lightly. God is coming to live among his people. Another reason for this lavish attention to detail is that the worship of God is central to Israel's identity. Exodus charts the course of this nation from slavery to worship, and servants of the great King will want to know every detail of his life in their midst. In Egypt, the Israelites had been forced to build for the pharaoh; now they willingly donate their materials and expertise to build God's house in their midst.

Between the two descriptions of the tabernacle, Exodus describes an episode of rebellion among the people against God and God's servant Moses (ch. 32). The people persuade Aaron, the high priest, to make and organize worship around an idol, a golden calf. God's dire reaction demonstrates how this apostasy threatens the covenant relationship itself, and Israel is saved from destruction through Moses' intercession. The second account of the tabernacle building (following the story of the golden calf) indicates that the Israelites' gracious and forgiving God remains committed to the covenant and will continue to live among the people in spite of their sin (34:6-7).

Exodus concludes with God's coming to dwell in the tabernacle (40:34-38). God's occasional appearances to Israel now yield to a permanent presence in their midst. God journeys with the people; the tabernacle moves with them wherever they go. It is an emblem of the full restoration of God's presence within the whole of creation, just as originally intended.

As the story of Exodus comes to a close, God has made considerable progress in the formation of the chosen people. God has entered a formal covenant relationship with them and they now have both the law and the tabernacle. Their life has been given both an ethical shape and a liturgical shape. What they need now is a place of their own.

But having God living in their midst is not going to be easy or straightforward. How are these sinful mortals going to cope with this awesome and holy Presence among them? After the golden calf incident, God reveals himself to Moses as compassionate and gracious, slow to anger, abounding in love and faithfulness, maintaining love to thousands and forgiving wickedness, rebellion, and sin (34:6-7). But God also says he does not leave the guilty unpunished. Indeed, the effects of the people's sin will reverberate to the third and fourth generations.

Leviticus: Living with a Holy God

Leviticus is all about the protocol for maintaining a right relationship with the King whose royal residence is within the Israelites' camp. The first seven chapters deal with the various kinds of sacrifices and offerings an Israelite can bring to the tabernacle and how these rituals are to be performed. So, for example, a person who sins unintentionally is to take a sin offering to the tabernacle and offer it there. By this offering the priest makes atonement for the offending party, and God grants forgiveness (Lev. 4:27-35). So as God takes up residence among the people, he graciously provides a way to maintain the relationship between him and them.

God's presence within the tabernacle and the structure of its worship takes place in a particular place. But this was never meant to detract from God's intention to be present in the entire life of the people. God's pervasive presence is the subject of the following chapters in Leviticus. In 10:10 the Lord alerts Aaron to the priestly responsibility to "distinguish between the holy and the common, between the unclean and the clean" in relation to animals, birds, different kinds of food, and various medical conditions.

For the modern reader, this seems an odd way of regulating life in relationship to God. The best way to understand all these regulations emerges from studies of how ancient cultures structured their lives. These seemingly random and strange regulations have profound symbolic significance for the Israelites. They remind Israel constantly, in every detail of personal and public life, of their special status as God's chosen people. They serve as a sort of sacrament that conveys the holiness of God and the holiness God expects from people in their daily lives.

The relationship of the holy God to the people comes to a dramatic climax in the description of the Day of Atonement (ch. 16). On this one day of the year, the high priest enters the Holy of Holies, the inner sanctuary of the tabernacle symbolizing the mercy seat of God. He brings sacrificial blood of animals representing the sacrifice needed for the atonement of the people's sins and sprinkles it on the "the mercy seat" (16:16, NRSV). This atonement ritual of ancient Israel will come to symbolize in a powerful way how God fully and finally atones for the sin of the world in Jesus Christ (Heb. 9).

Numbers: Journeying to the Land

At the conclusion of Leviticus, Israel is still at Mount Sinai. Numbers tells the story of their journey from there to the plains of Moab, just outside the promised land. Before they set off, God orders a census of Israelite men in each tribe who are over the age of twenty and able to serve in the army. God is shaping the ragtag group of slaves delivered from Egypt into a well-ordered unit ready for military conquest of the promised land. The total number of men is 600,000, which means that the total number of Israelites must be over two million. God had promised to make a great nation out of Abraham's descendants, and now Israel shows every sign of such emerging greatness.

Initially preparations for the journey go well. The first ten chapters of Numbers seem full of optimism as the Israelites make final preparations. This optimism is wonderfully captured in the priestly blessing that the Lord gives to Aaron and his sons as his own blessing upon Israel:

> The Lord bless you and keep you;
> The Lord make his face shine upon you and be gracious to you;
> The Lord turn his face toward you and give you peace (Num. 6:24-26).

In the Hebrew language, each line of this blessing is longer than the previous one, and the last line ends with the word "peace" (shalom). This is the goal of Israel's journey as the people set out for the promised land, for their God himself is going with them to lead the way.

Sadly, this optimism soon withers. Wilderness travel is not easy, and despite having God in their midst, the Israelites soon start moaning about their new hardships. God reacts in anger, sending fire out from the tabernacle that consumes parts of the camp (ch. 11). The Israelites call out to Moses for help. Only when he cries out to God on their behalf does the fire die down. Even after such a warning, the people continue to grumble, even complaining about the menu and the lack of meat in

> Wilderness travel is not easy, and despite having God in their midst, the Israelites soon start moaning about their new hardships.

their diet! Then there are difficulties among the leaders: Miriam and Aaron start to mutter about Moses' leadership and gossip about his marriage (ch. 12).

The biggest crisis in the story of the wilderness journey comes as Moses sends spies into the promised land, and they return with two reports (ch. 13-14). The majority report that the land is wonderfully fertile and would make a fine homeland for Israel, but that its people are powerful and their cities well fortified. When the people hear this report, their faith in the Lord collapses. Even though two of the spies encourage them to trust in God, they turn away, depressed and angry, complaining that God has brought them this far only to kill them. Once again, only Moses' intercession prevents God from destroying them all. God withholds immediate judgment but vows that none of this unbelieving generation will enter the promised land. So instead of claiming the new land immediately as God intended, the Israelites wander in the wilderness around Kadesh for forty years until the faithless first generation has died out.

After these forty tiring years, the Israelites finally come to the plains of Moab, just east of the promised land (ch. 22). Another census is taken to count the new generation of Israelites (ch. 26). The area west of the Jordan River is conquered and distributed among certain of the tribes (ch. 32), and Israel is poised to take possession of the promised land on the other side of the Jordan.

Deuteronomy: On the Borders of the Land

Even for this new generation of Israelites, it's going to be difficult to live up to God's covenant standards. But the land lies just ahead, and with it the possibility of rest and the fulfillment of God's promises to Abraham. Deuteronomy records the sermons Moses uses to equip the Israelites for their new task as they prepare to enter the land. These sermons present Israel with a vision of their calling as God's covenant people: a society brought together under the authority of the Lord alone, a people bound to God by his covenant with them, a people for the sake of the nations.

In his first sermon (Deut. 1:6-4:40), Moses reviews the recent history of the Israelites, the forty years since they left Sinai. He reminds the present generation of the important lessons to be

Israel's well-being as a people in the land will depend on their loving and serving God from the heart.

learned from their parents' experience. Their well-being as a people in the land will depend on their loving and serving God from the heart. The second sermon revisits in detail the law that is central to the covenant and expands it in relation to the Israelites' future life in the land. Moses reminds the Israelites of the Ten Words and then issues a powerful exhortation to love God by obeying these laws and making them absolutely central to their lives and their children's lives:

> Hear O Israel: The LORD our God, the LORD is one. Love the LORD your God with all your heart and with all your soul and with all your strength. These commandments that I give you today are to be upon your hearts. Impress them on your children. Talk about them when you sit at home and when you walk along the road, when you lie down and when you get up. Tie them as symbols on your hands and bind them on your foreheads. Write them on the doorframes of your houses and on your gates (6:4-8).

God's words are intended to instruct Israel in every area of life, for only then will Israel truly become a light to the nations. Religion is no merely private affair: God's law is to permeate every part of the people's experience.

Modern readers often find the instruction to drive out the other nations from the land difficult to stomach (Num. 33:50-54; Deut. 7). But this part of the biblical story does show sensitivity to the potential injustice inherent in the Israelites' conquest of lands that had been the home of other peoples. According to Genesis 15:16, God does not take the land away from its original inhabitants until their sin has reached such depths that they have in effect forfeited their right to it. The decision to disinherit them is just.

In fact, the behavior of the Canaanites reaches such depravity that judgment, when it does come at the hands of the Israelites, is long overdue. Because the Israelites must be fully committed to the Lord, the presence of other cultures with other gods alongside the people of Israel would present a constant temptation to idolatry, undermining Israel's identity as God's covenant people. This is why in Deuteronomy (as in 7:5; cf. Num. 33:52), the instruction to displace the former inhabitants of the land is part of the exposition of the first commandment: "You shall have no other gods." God applies at least as stern a judgment on his own people when they turn away from him to idolatry. The very land they conquer comes under the control of nations who now conquer them (see 2 Kings 17:5-8; 24).

Having reminded Israel of its covenant responsibilities, Moses sets before the people two options for their future. If they respond to God's word in faith and obedience they will experience life, prosperity, and blessing. If they respond in unbelief and disobedience they will face death, destruction, and curse (Deut. 27-28; 30:11-20). Moses urges the people to choose life and blessing by being obedient. Then he renews the covenant with them and appoints Joshua as his successor. God allows Moses to see the land of promise, though not to enter it. The book of Deuteronomy ends with Moses' death on the border of Canaan.

Reflections for Today

The apostle Peter describes the followers of Jesus Christ as "a chosen people, a royal priesthood, a holy nation, God's special possession" (1 Pet. 2:9). He then goes on to say that, though Jesus' disciples have become the people of God, they (we!) were not always such a people (2:10). We have followed the paths laid down by others. This is one clear indication of why it is so important for us here and now to know the story of God's ancient people of Israel. We do not stand alone before God in time and space. We stand within a history and tradition; we are part of a great ongoing story.

Peter did not invent those wonderful phrases he uses to describe Christians. They were first used in the Old Testament to describe the very people whose origins we have been tracing (Ex. 19:3-6). It will take the rest of the story to explain fully how their story came to be our story, but here is a quick preview:

- God calls Israel to be a model of what he intends for the whole of humankind;
- The Israelites cannot live up to God's calling because of their sin;
- Jesus takes up Israel's mission, not only modeling the kind of life that should characterize God's people but also, in his death and resurrection, atoning for the sin that always gets between us and God;
- Jesus calls together a new community who will at last truly become the people of God because their sin is forgiven through his sacrifice and their lives are filled with his own Spirit.

And this is where we come in. Though we are very different from the ancient people of Israel, it is the same God who calls us. Because we share the same calling, the same purpose, and the same mission, the life of ancient Israel teaches us, warns us, inspires us, and helps us to live as God's people and to understand God's ways. This connection between the ancient and modern people of God, spanning vast distances of space and time, is implicit even in the earliest biblical stories. Abraham was called to have a very special and personal relationship with God and to enjoy God's blessing on his own life. But God also intended these blessings to flow through Abraham to others who would come later. God's purpose is to restore the whole of creation, not just to salvage a bit from the wreckage of human rebellion.

Thus Abraham and his descendants become, by faith, those through whom God's blessings flow into human history. Each has a different faith experience—Abraham struggles to believe, Isaac meekly accepts his father's precepts, the independent and resourceful Jacob must learn not to rely on his own resources—but in each case it is their trust and belief in God's promises that brings them into relationship with God and calls them to be a channel of blessing to the nations.

In the remainder of Genesis and in Exodus, Leviticus, Numbers, and Deuteronomy—called the Pentateuch—the life of an entire nation comes into view, a people called to demonstrate what God wants for all humankind. Israel is called to be a nation whose life is so attractive that other nations will be drawn to them, and thus to the one true God. They are redeemed from slavery by God's direct intervention, bound to their loving Father in a covenant, and favored by God's own presence in their midst.

Those of us who follow Jesus see more continuity than strangeness between the experiences of ancient Israel and our own. We too have been redeemed—ransomed not out of Egyptian slavery but from slavery to sin. We too have entered into a covenant with God, not the Sinai covenant mediated by Moses but what Jesus called "the new covenant in [his] blood" (1 Cor. 11:25). Instead of a tabernacle and a pillar of cloud to

> **We too have been redeemed—ransomed not out of Egyptian slavery but from slavery to sin.**

remind us of God's presence in our lives, we have the living presence of the Holy Spirit within and among us. If we who come so late in the biblical story are to understand our own place in God's plan for the world, if we are indeed to be "a chosen people, a royal priesthood, a holy nation, God's special possession," we need to understand precisely this language of redemption, covenant, and presence—and the textbook of that language is the Pentateuch.

The unbelief and disobedience of God's people described in Numbers brings God's judgment and serves as a warning to God's people today to trust and obey (Heb. 3:8-19). Deuteronomy has much to teach us about life in covenant with God. This part of the story shows us God forming a people. We are now part of that people. Yet as the story continues we see that they fail in their calling. Only the work of Jesus to conquer the sin that pervaded Israel's life can form a people to be faithful to this calling. Israel's story teaches and warns. How will the Church carry out its calling?

Finding Our Place in the Story

1. Abraham was chosen by God to be a channel of blessing to others. If Christians were to take this up as their own responsibility in daily life, what difference would that make in your church?

2. Abraham, Isaac, and Jacob each had a relationship with God, but their faith journeys were quite different from one another. Can faith journeys today differ significantly as long as they are ultimately rooted in Christ? What elements of faith would most Christians agree to be basic to their relationship with God? In what ways do Christians' faith journeys differ in your experience?

3. Exodus shows that God's people are redeemed from slavery, are bound to God in covenant, and enjoy God's presence in the camp. How are each of these blessings true for Christians also? How are they different for us?

4. Though the Old Testament laws were given to help people live out God's perfect plan for humanity, they sometimes seem peculiar to us because they were written for a very different time and culture. If God were to give us a new set of laws for the time and place in which we live, what might he ask us to do in the following areas:

- justice
- selflessness
- joy
- thankfulness
- hope
- truth

5. The New Testament Church is reminded of Israel's unbelief and disobedience in the wilderness as a warning not to make the same mistakes (1 Cor. 10:1-13; Heb. 3:7-19). How does that story stand as a warning to us today?

6. Moses pleads with Israel to choose the path of life (Deut. 30:11-20). What are some ways in which secular culture has chosen a path of death? How can Christians choose the path of life?

Scene 2: A Land and a King for God's People

Joshua: The Gift of the Land

Having formed them in the wilderness, God now gives the people a land in which they can live and fulfill their call to be a display nation. The book of Joshua tells the story of the Israelites' conquest of Canaan under Joshua's leadership. Taking possession of their own land is a huge step forward in the story of the nation of slaves who left Egypt. Although the Israelites fight several battles, the narrative stresses throughout that the Israelites are entirely dependent upon the Lord for their success. Indeed, the land is a gift from the Lord fulfilling the promises to Abraham, Isaac, Jacob, and Moses.

Joshua prepares for the conquest by sending spies once again to survey the land. Their report doesn't have the tone of fear that dominated the report of the spies Moses sent forty years earlier into Canaan (Josh. 2; cf. Num. 13). Encouraged by this more favorable report, the Israelites set out for their new homeland. The ark of the covenant goes before them, holding back the waters of the Jordan and enabling them to cross. They erect a memorial of twelve stones taken from the riverbed to remind them that the Lord enabled them to cross this river and take possession of the land.

That this conquest is the Lord's work is illustrated in a vivid incident just west of the river near Jericho. An angel with a sword in his hand appears to Joshua. When Joshua asks him whose side he is on, the angel replies, "Neither, but as commander of the army of the LORD I have now come" (Josh. 5:13-15). Clearly, it is not Joshua but the Lord himself who is in charge of this campaign: the Lord alone will grant success.

The details of the conquest of Jericho repeatedly reinforce this concept. Under the Lord's instruction, the Israelites march around Jericho for seven days, with the ark (representing the presence of the Lord) leading the way. On the seventh day the walls of Jericho collapse at the sound of a trumpet and the shouting of the people. The Israelites then attack the city and destroy every living thing in it in obedience to the Lord's command (6:21). They spare only Rahab and her family, who have cooperated with their plans.

Several aspects of this "holy war" are hard for us to understand. Was it really necessary and just to kill all the citizens of Jericho and their animals? Yet God is quite clear in his instructions to the Israelites. (See a discussion of these issues on p. 68.) They *must* fight in this way. Indeed, their first attempt (just after their defeat of Jericho) to conquer the town of Ai ends in defeat precisely because one man, Achan of the tribe of Judah, disobeys God by keeping back some of the plunder from Jericho for himself (Josh. 7). This disobedience is taken

> Was it really necessary and just to kill all the citizens of Jericho and their animals?

very seriously and Achan is stoned to death. After this, the Israelites successfully conquer Ai (Josh. 8), but this time the Israelites are allowed to carry off the livestock and other goods from the city—as the Lord has instructed Joshua. The earlier problem at Ai caused by Achan's sin is a reminder that Israel would be successful in the land only if the people remain obedient to the Lord and keep the terms of his covenant.

After the conquest of Ai, Joshua fulfills Moses' commands in Deuteronomy 27:1-8 by renewing the covenant between the Lord and the Israelites (Josh. 8:30-35). The Israelites assemble on both sides of the ark of the covenant, half of them in front of Mount Gerizim and half in front of Mount Ebal. In the ceremony Joshua reads the law to the Israelites so that they clearly understand the options of blessing or curse that lie before them. God is giving the land to the Israelites so that they can live in it as God's people and be a light to the nations. But God will not tolerate behavior that is at odds with their calling. Israel would soon discover that failure to obey God is costly.

Chapters 9-12 tell the stories of the campaigns by which Joshua and the Israelites conquer the entire land. Near the end of this phase of conquest we read this summary: "Joshua took the entire land, just as the LORD had directed Moses, and he gave it as an inheritance to Israel according to their tribal divisions. Then the land had rest from war" (11:23). Chapters 13-19 tell how the land was allocated to each of the tribes of Israel. The inheritance of each tribe is assigned by lot (14:2-3).

The book of Joshua ends with the Israelites established in the land. This is an important milestone in the fulfillment of God's promises to Abraham. The promised land for Abraham's descendants has become a reality; the stage is set for Israel to live as a light to the nations. God's response to mutiny in his good creation was to elect one man, Abraham, and then to recover part of the earth and to place Abraham's descendants there. Now that Israel inhabits the land, they are to be a taste, a glimpse of what God intends for the whole of creation. Once more we are reminded of God's concern for the entire world.

This particular place on God's earth is a gift to the Israelites; Joshua describes it as "this good land" (23:15; cf. Deut. 6:10-11). It is pictured as a sort of second Eden. And like Adam and Eve in the garden, Israel is not free to exploit the land at will. They are to live in the land with the Lord, and God's laws instruct them how to manage the land and its people properly. In particular, the Sabbath laws serve as a powerful reminder that the Lord is the one who sustains the creation and that there is more to life than mere consumption. So even though it might be possible for a farmer in Israel to increase the yield of his crops slightly if he were to work his fields all seven days of the week, by obediently resting for one day each week, the farmer shows that he is trusting in God

> The Sabbath laws serve as a powerful reminder that the Lord is the one who sustains the creation and that there is more to life than mere consumption.

to prosper him. God promises, in his Sabbath laws, to honor such obedience with his blessing.

Will Israel live up to this challenge? Great and wonderful possibilities appear on the horizon. Joshua says that the land is to be the place of rest for the Israelites, but it is also a place of testing, of temptation. By no means are all of the Canaanites out of the land—that threat to peace remains. And the Israelites have too often shown their own disposition to rebel against the Lord and thus to forfeit his blessing. During Joshua's life the people do keep the covenant (Josh. 24:31), but their future in the land will depend on how they choose to live after Joshua's death. In his farewell speech to the leaders of Israel, Joshua reviews their history and exhorts them to decide whom to serve: the gods of the Amorites or the LORD God (24:15). The Israelites respond by committing themselves to serving the Lord, and Joshua renews the covenant with them, reminding them that the land is a gift from the Lord and that their future well-being depends on how they love and obey God.

The book of Joshua is an essential part of the biblical story and of our understanding of God's plan for the whole world. But as mentioned earlier, Joshua presents difficulties for the modern reader. Indeed, how we approach this book will have important implications for how we tell the whole story of the Bible. Even among Christians who do read the Bible as God's story, some see Jesus' teachings a radical contradiction to the "holy war" of the book of Joshua. Many modern readers find the wholesale destruction of Canaanites particularly hard to accept. Though we cannot entirely resolve these important issues, the story line of the Bible contains several clues that may help us to understand God's instructions to his people in the time of Joshua.

We have already recognized that God patiently waits until the evil in the land of Canaan has grown to a point at which God is compelled to judge its people (Gen. 15:16). Above all else, Israel's life must be characterized by the worship of God alone (the first commandment). Living among Canaanites, the Israelites are in danger of being lured into the worship of other gods.

We need to see this terrible call to drive out the pagan nations in the context of this struggle with idolatry. We tend not to take the dangers of idolatry so seriously today. But it doesn't take more than a cursory look at our situation as Christians in Western society to recognize the dangers of compromise with the idolatries of modern life. While we are to love our neighbors, we must be ruthless in rooting out idolatry from our personal and corporate lives. The key to understanding the command to drive out the Canaanites is to recall God's holiness and to realize just how much is at stake in the Israelites' remaining faithful to the Lord.

Judges: Failure to Be a Light to the Nations

Joshua is not replaced as leader of the Israelites. The expectation appears to be that the Israelites will live directly under the Lord's reign with some help from the elders appointed by Moses and Joshua. Government is decentralized, but Israel does not flourish under such a tribal system. The book of Judges tells what happens once Joshua and his generation have died. The story is not encouraging. Time and again the Israelites do what is evil in the eyes of the Lord, and the Lord hands them over to their enemies. Judges illustrates Israel's downward spiral into rebellion and disaster at every level as she fails her calling to be a holy nation.

The book of Judges begins by noting that Israel does not wage war against idolatry, failing to expel all the Canaanites from the land (Judg. 1). In Judges 2:1-5 the Lord pronounces judgment on the people for their refusal to wage war against pagan idolatry: God will not drive out the remaining pagan nations, and their idols will be a snare to Israel.

Thus the temptation to follow the old gods of Canaan remains. And the Israelites regularly succumb to the temptation, serving "the Baals" (2:11-13). Baal is a fertility god, and the plural indicates the many local manifestations of one god. The Israelites, unlike the Canaanites, are new to agriculture. The seductive attraction of Canaanite religion for the newcomers is its promise of fertility for the land and thus economic success. The Israelites fall for the gods that seem to deliver the goods immediately.

God's judgment is carried out in cycles that characterize Israel's life in the book of Judges:

- The Israelites sin by worshiping "the Baals and the Asherahs" (3:8), violating the covenant and provoking the Lord to anger.
- The Lord hands the Israelites over to their enemies.

- Under oppression by their enemies, the Israelites cry out to the Lord for deliverance.
- The Lord raises up a military leader (a judge) to deliver them from their oppression (2:11-19). All goes well for a while, but when the judge dies and the Israelites forget the lesson, they once more slide into idolatry and the whole sorry cycle is repeated.

The first judge mentioned is Othniel, younger brother of Caleb (Joshua's right-hand man). Because of Israel's apostasy, the Lord has "sold" the nation into the hands of Cushan, a foreign king (3:7-11). The Israelites chafe under his harsh rule for eight years. Then they cry out to the Lord, who raises up Othniel as a judge to rescue them. The Spirit of the Lord comes upon Othniel, and he delivers Israel from the grip of Cushan. Then Israel enjoys peace for forty years, until once again, "the Israelites did evil in the eyes of the LORD . . ." (v. 12).

The cycle of disobedience continues throughout the book, but the level of sin worsens until the circular pattern of disobedience—oppression, repentance, deliverance—becomes a downward spiral into chaos. Successive judges become more and more flawed, and the Israelites embrace debauchery, rape, and murder (ch. 19). At last the nation is plunged civil war. The last of the judges, Samson, is himself an image of what his nation has become: set apart for service to God, yet fatally attracted to paganism (ch. 13-16).

Samson is a Nazirite, an Israelite who has made "a vow of separation" to the Lord to abstain from certain things (such as wine) for a specified period. As a sign of his separation, a Nazirite would leave his hair uncut. The three areas prohibited to the Nazirite are fertility (symbolized by grape products),

> **Samson is himself an image of what his nation has become: set apart for service to God, yet fatally attracted to paganism.**

sympathetic magic, and the cult of the dead—and these are the main religious practices the Israelites are tempted to adopt from the Canaanites. Thus the separation of a Nazirite symbolizes for all Israelites how they should live holy lives apart from these pagan practices.

Separation and holiness should be hallmarks of a man like Samson, who is a Nazirite for life (13:4-7). And Samson indeed achieves great things for God, delivering the Israelites from the Philistines through many superhuman feats of strength. But Samson's own life is a mess. He marries one Philistine woman, consorts with prostitutes, and then is fatally attracted to yet another Philistine woman, Delilah (ch. 16). Through Delilah, the Philistines discover the secret of Samson's strength—his hair! While he is sleeping, Delilah has his hair cut off; when he awakens, his strength is gone. The Philistines gouge Samson's eyes out and throw him into prison.

But the Lord allows Samson his revenge against the Philistines. At a special feast, the Philistine rulers celebrate their god Dagon's power over the Israelites (and over the Israelites' God). For entertainment they have Samson brought before them and chain him to the pillars of the building. By now his hair has grown and his strength has returned, and in a last feat of strength, Samson pulls down the pagan temple on top of the crowd, taking his own life along with theirs. "Thus he killed many more when he died than while he lived" (16:30). It's a strange epitaph, and Samson's complex and often sordid life symbolizes what Israel itself has become. Yet God uses Samson's life and death to deliver Israel.

The book of Judges begins and ends with war. At its beginning the nation is engaged in a holy war; by the end of the book the Israelites are fighting one another. Throughout Judges we see the tendency of the Israelites to do "what [is] right in their own eyes" (17:6; 21:25, NRSV), rather than walking in God's own way of life. By the time of the last judge, Samson, even Israel's ruler habitually obeys no higher authority than his own corrupt will. Israel has all but forgotten the perfect standard of God's law.

Samuel: Israel Transformed into a Kingdom

The Need for a King

The book of Judges explains Israel's long descent into chaos in the final verse: "In those days Israel had no king; everyone did as they saw fit" (21:25). This raises an important question: What leadership does Israel need in order to live effectively as God's covenant people? Does Israel need a king? Of course, in one important sense Israel already has a king: the Lord. But what kind of human leadership will ensure that Israel remains faithful to the Lord?

The books of 1 and 2 Samuel start with the story of a barren woman and a barren nation. (It's interesting to note how often new advances in God's story begin in barrenness—Sarah, Rachel, and Samson's mother, to name a few.) The woman is Hannah. Like the Israelites, who at this time are being oppressed by their enemies, Hannah cries out to the Lord to take away the stigma of her infertility (1 Sam. 1). The nation too is barren in the sense that it is not producing the fruits of obedience to God's covenant. Even the formal worship of God in Israel has become corrupt; it has lost its sense of God's holiness. The sons of Eli the priest are scoundrels; they have "no regard for the LORD" (1 Sam. 2:12). The name of one of Eli's grandsons captures the seriousness of the situation: Ichabod means "the Glory has departed" (4:21). The true glory of the nation, God's presence among the Israelites, literally departs from them when the Philistines capture the ark of the covenant.

This "ark" is a highly decorated wooden box containing a copy of the Ten Words and thus symbolizing the living presence of God among the people. The Israelites have begun to treat it as if it were a magical charm, a way to bring God on their side when they are threatened by enemies. When Israel suffers a defeat in battle against the Philistines, they fetch the ark and carry it with them to the next skirmish in an effort to guarantee victory. Instead the Israelites are crushed. Thirty thousand of them are slaughtered and the ark itself is captured by the Philistines. In this rout, both of Eli's sons are killed, and Eli himself dies of shock and grief when he hears the dreadful news.

God's Kind of King

Though Israel has not actually been taken out of the land, God has departed from it and, symbolized by the capture of the ark, is living within the enemy camp! Once again, Israel's only hope is that God will return to them and bring new life out of their barrenness. And that is what happens: the ark's presence among the Philistines causes such havoc that they are desperately glad to let it return to Israel (1 Sam. 5-6).

God also begins a new chapter in the story as he answers Hannah's prayer, delivering her from her barrenness and at the same time delivering Israel from its lack of spiritual integrity. God gives Hannah a son, Samuel, who is also the last and greatest of the judges. Like Samson, Samuel is a Nazirite (1 Sam. 1:11, 24-28). But unlike Samson, Samuel is the genuine article. He is a charismatic leader who courageously delivers Israel from its enemies and wisely settles disputes among the Israelites themselves. Samuel is both judge and priest, and he is also honored as a prophet because of his reliable words (3:19-20) and his integrity (12:3-4).

Samuel also bears some similarity to Moses in that he too admonishes the Israelites to turn away from idols and serve the Lord from their hearts (ch. 12). But perhaps his greatest role is as the God-appointed kingmaker. Though his own sons Joel and Abijah are appointed to be judges in Samuel's old age, they turn out to be more like Eli's sons than like their own father. So the leaders of the tribes of Israel come to Samuel and request a king "such as all the other nations have" (8:1-5).

These few words generate a heated debate among Samuel, God, and the elders of Israel, for the question of who should lead the people is central to the very identity of Israel (ch. 8). If Israel is to be a light to the nations and bring blessing to them, then it must be set apart from them. But in asking for a king such as the other nations have, Israel seems to want to be like those other nations. Samuel complains to the Lord, who has him warn the Israelites about the dangers of a human king (8:11-18; cf. Deut. 17:14-20). But the Israelites are adamant: they want a king to lead them and to provide military success, and they express no desire to live more obediently as God's covenant people. At last the Lord tells Samuel to listen to the Israelites and anoint Saul as king over Israel.

Although the details are not spelled out, we are told that Samuel explains to the Israelites the "rights and duties of kingship," which he writes down and places in the tabernacle before the Lord (1 Sam. 10:25; cf. Deut. 17:18-20). Because Samuel's prophetic messages from God provide a check on the king's power, kingship in Israel (by design) remains compatible with the covenant. Samuel's prophetic role is clearly designed to provide a system of checks and balances in relation to the emerging kingship in Israel. The struggle between prophecy and kingship, between spiritual goals and political aims, characterizes the subsequent history of Israel until the exile.

> The struggle between prophecy and kingship, between spiritual goals and political aims, characterizes the subsequent history of Israel until the exile.

Lest Israel lose its distinctive nature, Israel must not only have a king but a theology of kingship. The Lord is the one who chooses the king, has him anointed by Samuel, and endows him with the Spirit. Only then is the king publicly attested before Israel. Thus its human kings are firmly established as ruling under the great King, the Lord. When Samuel the prophet anoints the king of Israel, that mortal king becomes the Lord's Messiah ("anointed one"; 2:10; 10:1; 16:13).

Saul Rules Unfaithfully

Under Saul's leadership, Israel achieves significant military success against the Philistines. But Saul's disobedience to God compromises his career until eventually God must remove Saul from the throne, as Samuel prophesies: "Because you have rejected the word of the LORD, he has rejected you as king" (1 Sam. 15:23).

Under God's direction, Samuel seeks out the future king and anoints him: he is David, a young man from Bethlehem. From this time onward Saul becomes more and more mentally unhinged; David rises to prominence as Saul declines. The Spirit comes upon David but departs from Saul (16:13-14). David's military success in defeating Goliath and the Philistines draws him to Saul's attention, and Saul's son Jonathan becomes David's devoted friend. David also marries Saul's daughter Michal. As a skilled musician, David provides comfort for Saul during the king's periods of mental turmoil, but later he becomes a target of the older man's manic anger.

David's growing reputation as a military leader particularly inflames Saul's jealousy. Hearing the Israelite women chanting "Saul has slain his thousands, and David his tens of thousands" is too much for Saul, and he tries to kill David (18:7-11). The younger man becomes a fugitive with a band of outlaws roaming the countryside. But God blesses David with a further string of military successes. During this period David has several opportunities to kill Saul, but he refuses to lift up a hand against "the LORD's anointed" (24:6).

Saul's forty-year reign ends after several unsuccessful attempts to have his appointed successor murdered. Desperate because of God's silence, Saul even consults a spirit medium for advice about dealing with the military threat from the Philistines (ch. 28). At the end of 1 Samuel, facing the defeat of his own army at the hands of the Philistines, Saul takes his own life (ch. 31).

This is not an auspicious start for the monarchy in Israel. The grim history of Saul points out how the institution of the human monarch is dangerous for

Israel. One thing is clear: God wants a king to rule under him who understands that God alone is the ultimate sovereign over Israel. The human king under God's own divine kingship must enable the Israelites to live up to their covenant calling to be a light to the nations. This is why God must deal decisively with the disobedience of Israel's first human king.

The story of the rise and decline of kingship is told in three Old Testament double books: Samuel, Kings, and Chronicles. From the story of Saul's death on, Chronicles covers the same ground as Samuel and Kings. It is widely accepted that Samuel and Kings are intended as a single, progressive narrative and that Chronicles is a distinctly separate work; thus we have two points of view on this part of the biblical story.

David Rules Faithfully

After the deaths of Saul and Jonathan, war breaks out between the houses of David and Saul, but David's faction grows steadily stronger. Judah (the southern part of the nation of Israel) first chooses David as king (2 Sam. 2:1-7) and then all of Israel agrees with this choice (5:1-4). David enjoys further military victory against the Philistines and begins to consolidate his rule. He brings the ark of the covenant of God to Jerusalem, which is to be both David's own city and the fixed place where God himself will dwell among the people. David builds his palace in Jerusalem and then wants to build a home for the Lord too. But Nathan the prophet reveals that it is not for David himself to do this, rather David's son and successor. The Lord does confirm David as king and promises to establish him and his heirs to reign over Israel.

In his covenant with David (7:5-16) God promises

- to make David's name great;
- to provide a secure place for his people Israel;
- to give them rest from their enemies;
- to establish David's dynasty;
- to enable David's son to build "a house" for God;
- to establish the throne of David's forever.

Responding to God with thanksgiving and worship, David places these promises clearly in relation to the promises made long ago to Abraham (7:18-29). With this new covenant with David, God officially constitutes Israel as a kingdom, and Israel can now fulfill its calling to be a light to the nations as a kingdom. Israel's human king will lead the people to be a holy nation and priestly kingdom as he removes idolatry from the land and gives Israel rest and shalom.

At first under King David's reign Israel enjoys a time of rest and peace. A fabulously successful warrior, David soon secures Israel's borders. He reigns "over all Israel, doing what [is] just and right for all his people" (8:15). He is generous in victory, showing kindness to Saul's relatives, as when he welcomes Jonathan's crippled son Mephibosheth into his family and gives him the property of his grandfather Saul.

But although David is God's anointed king, he also reveals his human sinfulness. The remainder of 2 Samuel records a catalogue of his sins and errors in judgment. David commits adultery with Bathsheba and then conspires to have her husband murdered. But Nathan the prophet comes to know of these things and confronts David with a parable with a real sting in its tail (ch. 11-12). He tells David a story of a rich man, the owner of many flocks, and a poor man who owns just one lamb, a family pet. When the rich man needs a special meal for a visiting guest, he arrogantly slaughters the poor man's lamb instead of one of his own. This tale of greed and injustice so angers King David that he vows to visit terrible punishments on the "rich man." Then Nathan turns on the king and declares, "You are the man!" David has acted out of arrogance and greed in taking another man's wife.

Convinced of his sin, David weeps, repents before God, and is forgiven (cf. Ps. 51). But his actions bear tragic consequences. The child conceived in David's adulterous union with Bathsheba dies. Rape, murder, and rebellion erupt in David's own extended family. God's judgment on David reaches its climax with the death of his beloved son Absalom (see below).

The book of 2 Samuel ends with God giving a positive answer to David's plea for an end to famine. This is a sure sign of reconciliation between the king and the Lord. In the short evaluative notes given in 1 and 2 Kings concerning each of the kings who come after Solomon, David is invariably the standard by which each king's reign is measured.

David is invariably the standard by which each king's reign is measured.

For example, King Abijah's "heart was not fully devoted to the LORD his God, as the heart of David his forefather had been" (1 Kings 15:3).

The primary interest of the biblical writer is to show how each of the kings relates to the Lord; the author cares little for other kingly accomplishments such as grand building projects. Though we know from other historical sources that King Omri achieved great things in architecture and nation-building, the book of Kings dismisses him in a few verses as a king who displeases the Lord. David, by contrast, is depicted as genuinely devout. Throughout the Old Testament his name is closely associated with the Psalms, many of which he may have written. They reveal a profound spirituality in this surprisingly complicated man and king. Historians of Israel call David the "man after God's own heart" (1 Sam. 13:14). He serves as an example of the best we humans can do, hobbled as we are by our sinful hearts.

As we have seen, nothing about Israel's experiment with monarchy is straightforward. Every step seems fraught with difficulties, and this is true also of King David's succession. God's promise to establish David's line forever does little to prevent power struggles among his heirs. After David's son Absalom builds up a military force, he seizes the throne and forces David to flee for his life (2 Sam. 15), but in the course of the ensuing battle, Absalom himself is killed. At Bathsheba's request, David finally declares his son Solomon as heir to the throne and thereby establishes his dynasty (1 Kings 1).

David's kingship, flawed as it was, remains a key to understanding the ongoing story of how God reestablishes his kingdom. God promised to establish David's kingdom foreverd. "Your house and your kingdom will endure forever before me . . . ." (2 Samuel 7:16) That "forever" kingdom would come many years in the future as the one who was called David's son as well as the Son of God came to announce his kingdom.

Kings: Covenant Failure

Solomon Begins His Rule Wisely

If David is best known for his trust in the Lord and his profound spirituality, Solomon is renowned for his wisdom. When he offers a thousand burnt offerings to the Lord at Gibeon, the Lord responds by offering the young prince whatever he asks for. Solomon declares himself inadequate for the task of being king and requests "a discerning heart to govern [God's] people and to distinguish between right and wrong" (1 Kings 3:9). Pleased with this request, the Lord promises Solomon the wisdom he asks for, as well as riches and honor. Solomon's wisdom becomes legendary: he is an expert in proverbial wisdom and has extensive knowledge of plants, animals, reptiles, and fish (4:29-34). He is also credited with establishing a structure of government for Israel (4:1-19).

The Old Testament includes several books of "wisdom": Proverbs, Ecclesiastes, and Job. The association of Proverbs and Ecclesiastes with Solomon indicates the sort of thinking he initiated in the cultural and religious life of Israel. In these books, wisdom is all about knowing how to live effectively, how to express God's glory in a good (though fallen) world. Wisdom is conforming oneself to the order God established in creation. It begins with "the fear of the LORD," a profound reverence for the Lord as God the Creator and Redeemer (Prov. 1:7)—precisely the sort of attitude Solomon manifests in recognizing himself as a fallible, limited human creature, utterly dependent upon God.

"The fear of the Lord" is also the starting point for a journey of exploration that extends throughout the whole creation. The foundation of wisdom is recognizing that the Lord is God the Creator: the very fabric of creation comes from God. So those who serve the Lord wisely will take seriously the whole of creation in all its magnificent variety.

> **The foundation of wisdom is recognizing that the Lord is God the Creator: the very fabric of creation comes from God.**

This is precisely what Solomon does: his wisdom shows itself in the study of plants, reptiles, animals, and fish, and in the study of how to use language to sum up insight in short, pithy aphorisms. In the book of Proverbs there is no area of life that wisdom does not reflect upon, including family life, sexuality, politics, economics, business, and law. Indeed, it ends with a powerful portrait of wisdom incarnate in the woman "of noble character" who manifests her fear of the Lord in a truly extraordinary variety of activities (Prov. 31).

Solomon Establishes the Temple in Zion

Solomon's greatest achievement is constructing God's permanent temple in Jerusalem to replace the tabernacle, using only the best materials and sparing no cost. The ark is brought into the temple to mark the fulfillment of the Israelites' journey out of bondage in Egypt. The Lord and Israel are now at rest in the land. When the ark is deposited in the temple, the exodus cloud fills the temple, showing that the glory of the Lord is present in Jerusalem (1 Kings 8:11). Once again God has an address on earth among people.

In the huge dedication ceremony, Solomon specifically relates the founding of the temple to the fulfillment of God's ancient promises to Israel. Before this, the Lord had not settled in one place in Israel. Now Jerusalem is chosen as God's city and the temple as a place "for the Name of the LORD" (8:19-21; cf. Deut. 12.5). In his prayer of dedication, Solomon acknowledges that the heavens themselves can never contain God, much less a building made by human hands. However, as the cloud descending to the inner sanctuary of the temple alerts us, the God of glory is truly present in the midst of his people. Solomon asks God that the temple may be a place where the Israelites can pray and be heard by God. God's presence in the temple signifies God's close relationship to the people.

Solomon's time is marked by great fulfillment of promises. Israel is now a cohesive nation living in its promised homeland, and the Lord dwells in its midst. For these things Solomon gives thanks: "Praise be to the LORD, who has given rest to his people Israel just as he promised. Not one word has failed of all the good promises he gave through his servant Moses" (1 Kings 8:56). Jerusalem is established as the capital of Israel, with the temple and the King's residence within its walls. This marks a new chapter in the story of Israel.

Jerusalem (or "Zion," as it is also known) fires the imagination of the prophets and leaders of Israel in the time of Solomon and after. The city with God's temple in it is celebrated in much of Israel's poetry:

> Great is the Lord, and most worthy of praise,
> in the city of our God, his holy mountain.
> Beautiful in its loftiness,
> the joy of the whole earth,
> like the heights of Zaphon is Mount Zion,

the city of the Great King.

God is in her citadels;

he has shown himself to be her fortress (Ps. 48:1-3).

Great is the LORD in Zion; he is exalted over all the nations (Ps. 99:2).

Jerusalem becomes the center for Israel's formal worship, and the Israelites make regular pilgrimages to it, pilgrimages that inspire the psalms of ascent (Ps. 120-134). As we read these poems, we need to imagine pilgrims approaching Jerusalem—the Lord's own dwelling place—reciting, "I lift up my eyes to the mountains—where does my help come from? My help comes from the LORD, the Maker of heaven and earth" (121:1-2). As they approach Jerusalem, the pilgrims look to the hills of Jerusalem and reflect on the source of their help. These pilgrims know well that the Lord, who has a local "address" in this city and is their constant helper, is also the Creator of the whole world.

To bring their messages to Israel, the prophets too would use the imagery of Zion again and again. Unfortunately, as we will see, this was often because things in Jerusalem were not going well during the time of the prophets. But in Solomon's great day at the dedication of the temple, it must have seemed as though Eden itself had been recovered. Shalom and great blessing lay before Israel. The monarchy appeared to have brought peace and prosperity in a measure that Samuel and other critics of the institution of kingship could not have dreamt of. Now perhaps Israel could begin to draw the nations to God.

The Kingdom Is Torn in Two

Sadly, the seeds of civil strife and apostasy already present in Solomon's day soon bring a deadly harvest. First, Solomon does not oppose the worship of God at the "high places" where the Baals had been worshiped, despite the danger of apostasy. Second, he begins to use forced labor to fulfill his ambitious building plans. Third, he takes foreign wives. The first and third of these leave the kingdom vulnerable to idolatry, and such idolatry starts to pollute Israel as Solomon grows older. His use of forced labor begins to alienate the people, and at the time of Solomon's death their resentment has become intense. More importantly, the Lord becomes angered by Solomon's idolatry (1 Kings 11:33), which violated the heart of the covenant. God therefore tells Solomon that he will tear much of the kingdom away from Solomon's heirs, leaving only two tribes, Judah and Benjamin, to be ruled by his successor (11:13, 36).

True to God's word, after Solomon's death the nation splits into a northern kingdom (called Israel) under King Jeroboam and a southern kingdom (called Judah) under King Rehoboam. The rebellion of the northern tribes against Solomon's heir comes in explicit response to Solomon's policy of using forced labor. When Rehoboam rejects the northern tribes' request to lighten the burden of forced labor, the kingdoms separate. The political consequences of this schism are immense (ch. 12). The nation of Israel is now divided against itself, and both kingdoms are far more vulnerable to their enemies. Soon each begins to regard the other as an enemy.

After the separation, how can the northern kingdom remain true to the Lord, who "lives" in the south, in Jerusalem? Jeroboam (the northern king) has a religious problem with political and military implications. Jeroboam risks losing control of his own kingdom if he allows his subjects to travel south to the temple in Judah's territory for worship. To avoid this, Jeroboam embraces idolatry. He repeats the sin of the Israelites at Sinai (Ex. 32) by having two golden calves made and set up in sanctuaries at Dan and Bethel (1 Kings 12:26-33). This is an ominous beginning for the northern kingdom, and its subsequent history has apostasy written all over it. Through the prophet Ahijah, God rejects Jeroboam, principally because of the idolatry of his kingdom (ch. 14).

Elijah and Elisha Confront an Unfaithful Israel

From this point in Israel's story, the role and message of the prophets become increasingly important. (The word "prophet" literally means one who speaks for, in this case, God.) Throughout Israel's history, God's word has played a key role, whether it has come through Moses or Samuel or another prophet. However, as the office of king becomes firmly established in Israel, the office of prophet becomes more clearly delineated from other public roles. All the prophetic books in the Old Testament come from the time of the monarchy or after its demise. The prophetic office thus appears in Israel as a counterbalance to the powerful office of king.

> There is no dynasty of prophets; each is called separately to bring God's word to Israel and especially to its leaders at a specific moment in the nation's history.

There is no dynasty of prophets; each is called separately to bring God's word to Israel and especially to its leaders at a specific moment in the nation's history. Israel is a theocracy, and God's word, not the word of the human king, has final authority. For that reason we often find a prophet in bitter confrontation with the king of his day. For example, when Jeroboam's son is ill, he sends his wife to consult Ahijah. This prophet then has the unenviable task of telling King Jeroboam's wife that her son will die as soon as she steps back into her city. And this death will be preferable to the judgment that is about to happen to the rest of Jeroboam's house (1 Kings 14:15).

But God is patient and longsuffering and does not quickly cast the northern kingdom into exile. Sadly, the kings who follow Jeroboam are much like him in their sin. Events in the north reach their nadir when Ahab takes the throne of Israel. Ahab marries Jezebel, a foreigner who brings Baal worship with her into the marriage and into the northern kingdom. Their rebellion against God is utterly brazen. In this context of radical apostasy, God calls Elijah the prophet to confront Ahab in the name of the Lord. Underlying the struggle between Elijah and Ahab is the more fundamental conflict between Baal and the Lord: to which "god" will the north give its allegiance?

This conflict leads to a dramatic public contest between Baal and the Lord on the top of Mount Carmel. Elijah assembles the people and appeals to them to make up their minds and hearts: "If the LORD is God, follow him; but if Baal is God, follow him" (18:21). The people remain quiet and so Elijah has two bulls sacrificed and declares that the true God will send fire from heaven to consume one of the sacrifices. The prophets of Baal cry out to their gods all day, but there is no answer. Elijah then builds an altar with twelve stones to represent the twelve tribes of Israel. Wood and the sacrificial bull are placed on the altar and water is poured over it all. At the time of the evening sacrifice, Elijah prays to the "LORD, the God of Abraham, Isaac and Israel." When the Lord sends fire that consumes the sacrifice and the altar, the people fall on their faces and cry out, "The LORD—he is God!" (18:39).

We need to understand Elijah's ministry, and that of Elisha, who follows him, in the context of this life-and-death clash between Baal and the Lord. Through Elijah and Elisha, the Lord overcomes drought (18:41-46), hunger (17:8-16), thirst (2 Kings 2:19-22), debt (4:1-7), infertility (4:11-17), disease (5:1-19), and death (1 Kings 17:17-24; 2 Kings 4:18-37). Baal worshipers believed these areas of life to be under Baal's control. Elijah and Elisha show that the Lord God alone is king of his people, of every aspect of their lives, and indeed of the whole creation.

The blessings that come from the Lord through the prophets are not limited to Israel. When Naaman, a commander in the army of Aram (Syria), suffers from leprosy and comes in desperation to Elisha for healing, God answers his prayer (2 Kings 5). Naaman then takes away with him as much earth from Israel as two mules can carry, so that he can worship the Lord on "the land" of promise—even after he has returned to his own country of Aram! Here is a wonderful example of Israel's bringing blessing to the nations. Sadly, Israel itself becomes more and more like the surrounding pagan nations because the people refuse to serve the Lord alone.

Israel's Steady Slide toward Disaster and Exile

Much of 2 Kings tells the stories of the northern and southern kingdoms in something like a split-screen presentation with the two stories running side by side. In the north, Jehu is called by God and anointed by Elisha with the specific instruction to wipe out Ahab's house (ch. 9). This he does, but also maintains the worship of the golden calves and the traditions of Jeroboam. Israel continues to slide steadily toward disaster. Assyria is the great Middle Eastern empire of the day and its shadow falls increasingly on the northern kingdom. During the reign of Israel's King Hoshea, Assyria invades the northern kingdom, lays siege to its capital, Samaria, for three years, and then deports the northern tribes of Israel to Assyria in 722 BC (ch. 17). This marks the end of the northern kingdom.

The narrator in 2 Kings pauses at this point for a lengthy reflection on why such a thing has happened to Israel. The exile raises the most fundamental questions in the minds of faithful Israelites. Wasn't the land a gift from the Lord himself? How then could he have allowed his people to be taken from it? Where are God's promises? What will happen now to Judah, the southern kingdom? Has God abandoned his vows to Abraham, Moses, and David?

The answers to these questions come in 2 Kings 17:7-23. The Lord has punished the northern kingdom in this way because of its disobedience to the covenant. Though God had repeatedly warned the people through his prophets of the consequences of idolatry, they persisted in their sin and rebellion. So "the LORD . . . removed them from his presence" (17:18). The exile comes not as a result of Assyria's power but because the Lord will no longer withhold judgment.

> The exile comes not as a result of Assyria's power but because the Lord will no longer withhold judgment.

Ominously, the narrator notes that Judah, the southern kingdom, has not behaved very differently (17:19). But Judah continues unconquered and the monarchy there fares much better than the northern kings ever had. In the years following 722 BC, the story highlights two outstanding kings in Judah—Hezekiah and Josiah—who seek to honor the Lord. Is there still hope for Judah, since the Davidic line rules? Hezekiah's reign parallels Hoshea's in the north. But when Assyria also threatens Hezekiah, he (unlike Hoshea) casts himself upon the Lord. With God's aid, mediated through the prophet Isaiah, Hezekiah holds firm and Judah is miraculously delivered from the Assyrian threat (ch. 18-19; cf. Isa. 8:6-10).

But signs of serious trouble appear even in Hezekiah's reign. As Assyria wanes, Babylon emerges as the new international power. Hezekiah's folly in showing Babylonian envoys around his storehouses evokes an oracle of judgment from the prophet Isaiah: the southern kingdom too will go into exile; Babylon will conquer Judah (2 Kings 20:12-19). Many of the prophecies in Isaiah 1-39 chronicle the ambiguity of these times in which Judah is, on the whole, a sinful nation heading for judgment.

King Manasseh, Hezekiah's successor, promotes idolatry and syncretism and is renowned for perpetuating injustice in his kingdom. Judah's doom seems inevitable.

Then Manasseh's grandson Josiah suddenly becomes king—at only eight years of age! While still a young man, Josiah hears a newly discovered law book being read aloud in the temple and is greatly moved by what he hears. Josiah then leads the people of Judah in public repentance, renews God's covenant with them, and embarks on a major reform of worship. Josiah pleases the Lord in this respect and is commended for his reign.

But even Josiah's exemplary leadership is too little too late for Judah. From the prophet Jeremiah we know that the reforms instituted by Josiah probably are not widely embraced and the tendency toward apostasy remains. Babylon's shadow hangs more and more over Judah. During Zedekiah's reign, Babylon conquers the southern kingdom and sets fire to the temple and the king's palace. Jerusalem is reduced to ruins and most of Judah's people are exiled to Babylon in 587-586 BC (2 Kings 25).

At this point as we follow the biblical story of Israel we might well be tempted to write "The End" (cf. Ezek. 7:1-2). It certainly must have seemed like the end to the Israelites being marched off as slaves to Babylon. What had become of God's great promises to Abraham, of the covenant with Israel at Sinai, of the vow that David's house would go on forever? The temple of God had been destroyed. Where was the Lord while Babylon triumphed over Israel? Had God's purposes for the people finally run into the sand? Worse, had God's purposes to redeem the creation through Israel failed?

Israel's only hope for answers to these terrible questions was in the Lord. That's what makes the voices of the prophets so important in the biblical story and in our understanding of Israel's shifting fortunes. The Israelites have been defeated and crushed as a result of their disobedience—but *Yahweh* is still the Lord, and God's purposes endure. In the centuries leading up to Israel's expulsion from the land, its history has been regularly interpreted by the voices of God's prophets. These voices do not become silent with the exile. The apparent end of Israel as a nation does not end God's reign and his purposes.

The double book of Kings concludes on a tentative note of hope: King Jehoiachin of Judah is released from prison in Babylon and eats at the table of the king of Babylon (2 Kings 25:27-30). Perhaps the story of Israel is not quite finished. And yet Israel's surest hope for a future lies not in the chronicles of its history but in the writings of its prophets.

The Voices of the Prophets

We have already looked briefly at the ministries of Elijah and Elisha in the ninth century BC. Hosea too (in the eighth century) prophesies to the northern kingdom in powerful and moving ways. He compares Israel to a wife who has become a prostitute—and yet her husband cannot give her up. He agonizes over her and longs for her to return to him and to be a faithful spouse. In this way the horror of adultery becomes a metaphor for what Israel is committing against the Lord.

Amos, another prophet of the ninth and eighth centuries BC, is a shepherd called by the Lord to become a prophet to both the northern and southern kingdoms. Amos's preaching is highly creative and his message altogether devastating. He portrays the Lord as a lion about to pounce on his prey (Amos 1:2). In an extraordinary sermon (1:3-2:16), Amos denounces Israel's neighbors one by one. You can almost hear a loud "Amen!" from Israel as Damascus, Gaza, Tyre, Edom, Ammon, and Moab are condemned in turn. Then comes the twist: Amos moves on to Judah and Israel, denouncing them because they too have rejected the Lord's instruction and are full of idolatry and injustice. They too will suffer terrible judgment. (The "amens" likely cease here.)

Jeremiah and Ezekiel prophesy to Judah during its expulsion from the land. Jeremiah begins his ministry in King Josiah's reign, warning the people of Judah against trusting in mere symbols of God's presence such as the temple. The Lord tells Jeremiah to stand at the entrance of the temple, to warn them against a false trust in ritual:

> This is what the LORD Almighty, the God of Israel, says: Reform your ways and your actions, and I will let you live in this place. Do not trust in deceptive words and say, "This is the temple of the LORD, the temple of the LORD, the temple of the LORD!" If you really change your ways and your actions and deal with each other justly, if you do not oppress the foreigner, the fatherless or the widow and do not shed innocent blood in this place, and if you do not follow other gods to your own harm, then I will let you live in this place, in the land I gave to your ancestors for ever and ever. But look, you are trusting in deceptive words that are worthless (Jer. 7:3-8).

Such sermons are never popular, and Jeremiah suffers terrible opposition even as he agonizes over his message to the southern kingdom. The extent of his agony and struggle is evident in his personal prayers, which are scattered throughout his writings. In chapter 15, Jeremiah tells of how he once "ate" God's words with joy and delight, but now his pain is unending and his wound grievous and incurable (vv. 16, 18). It is certainly no easy thing to be God's prophet!

The message of all these prophets is that unless the people repent and return to God and obey him, judgment will come. The prophets begin to speak ominously of the "day of the Lord." No longer is this anticipated as a day of blessing and judgment on Israel's enemies; instead it is to be a day of judgment for Israel itself. As we saw above, that "day" does come, first for the northern kingdom of Israel (in 722 BC) and then for the southern kingdom of Judah (in 587-586 BC).

Ezekiel ministers among the exiles in Babylon itself. He depicts the glory of the Lord departing from Jerusalem (Ezek. 10) and interprets for the Israelites the meaning of what has happened to them in the exile.

Prophets such as Ezekiel insist that the exile is not "the end." The Lord's purposes remain, as do his covenant promises to Abraham, to Moses, and to David. The oracles of judgment from the prophets are mercifully interspersed with oracles of hope and a brighter future for God's people. Thus Jeremiah promises that the nation will return from exile and will once again occupy the land of promise. He looks forward to a time when, as God says,

> I will make a new covenant
> with the house of Israel
> and with the house of Judah. . . .
> I will put my law in their minds
> and write it on their hearts.
> I will be their God,
> and they will be my people. . . .
> They will all know me . . . (Jer. 31:31, 33-34).

The Catastrophe of Exile in Babylon

Because the land and the temple were such important symbols of Israel's nationhood and its identity as the people beloved of God, exile was a catastrophic experience. The instruments of exile were the great powers of the day: first Assyria, then Babylon. After the fall of Assyria (in 612 BC), Babylon gained control of the Near East. Nebuchadnezzar, king of Babylon (605-562), defeated the Egyptians at Carchemish in 605; he and his successors maintained their dominance until Cyrus of Persia defeated the Babylonians in 539. After the battle of Carchemish, the southern kingdom of Judah became subject to Babylon, but some years later, King Jehoiakim of Judah rebelled against his Babylonian overlords (2 Kings 24). Nebuchadnezzar then besieged Jerusalem and took Jehoiakim's successor Jehoiachin off to Babylon as a prisoner. Ten years later, Zedekiah (puppet king of Judah whom Nebuchadnezzar had appointed) also rebelled against Babylon. Once more Nebuchadnezzar returned to Jerusalem, but this time his army destroyed the city and the temple and took most of Jerusalem's citizens to Babylon (587-586 BC; 2 Kings 25). So the Lord used the ungodly empires of Assyria and Babylon as instruments of judgment upon his people Israel.

We should not think that the Lord was quick to cast people out of the land. On the contrary, God is portrayed throughout the Old Testament as moving slowly and regretfully toward this judgment. Hosea forcefully conveys the agony God endures in coming to the decision to eject Israel from the land: "How can I give you up, Ephraim? How can I hand you over, Israel?" (Hos. 11:8). The Old Testament prophets bear ample witness to God's patience with his people and to God's repeated efforts to call them back to faithfulness within the covenant.

The Old Testament prophets bear ample witness to God's patience with his people and to God's repeated efforts to call them back to faithfulness within the covenant.

Habakkuk prophesies to the southern kingdom as Babylon's influence casts a shadow over its life. When the prophet asks how God can stand by and allow injustice and violence to prosper in Judah, he gets a most surprising answer: God is going to use the Babylonians to punish Israel! In the rest of his oracles, Habakkuk wrestles with God, struggling to come to terms with what God is going to do. Finally, though God's ways remain mysterious to him, the prophet arrives at a place of trust:

I heard and my heart pounded,
my lips quivered at the sound;
decay crept into my bones,
and my legs trembled.
Yet I will wait patiently for the day of calamity
to come on the nation invading us.
Though the fig tree does not bud
and there are no grapes on the vines,
though the olive crop fails
and the fields produce no food,
though there are no sheep in the pen
and no cattle in the stalls,
yet I will rejoice in the LORD,
I will be joyful in God my Savior (Hab. 3:16-18).

Just how catastrophic the exile was for the Israelites is clear from the psalms of this period and from the book of Lamentations. Psalm 80 cries out to God about Jerusalem: "Why have you broken down its walls so that all who pass by pick its grapes? Boars from the forest ravage it and wild animals feed on it" (vv. 12-13). The book of Lamentations is a series of carefully structured laments that give poetic expression to the profound grief experienced by the exiles as they are forced to leave the land. Lamentations articulates Israel's grief, acknowledges the Lord's justice in judgment, and appeals to God to bring restoration and a future to Israel. These poems depict the heart-wrenching reality of the exile: "The roads to Zion mourn, for no one comes to her appointed festivals. All her gateways are desolate, her priests groan, her young women grieve, and she is in bitter anguish" (Lam. 1:4).

Paradoxically, these writings also offer a glimmer of hope to the Israelites in exile. Lamentations gives shape to their grief and, with its focus on the Lord, holds out the possibility of renewal and restoration. This kind of

> In exile Israel learns that its God is far more than his earthly "house," far greater than the nation itself. God is truly the Lord of the nations, the Lord of all creation.

literature was crucial to Israel's survival as a nation. Without hearing God's voice through the prophets, the Israelites would not have maintained their sense of God's claim upon them as his own people. Although the temple had been razed, in exile Israel learns that its God is far more than his earthly "house," far greater than the nation itself. God is truly the Lord of the nations, the Lord of all creation. Though the people might suffer exile in Babylon, God is not conquered.

Though some of the exiles hope for a quick return from Babylon to their own land, the prophets dash this hope. Once Jerusalem falls in 587-586 BC), prophets such as Jeremiah and Ezekiel concentrate on comforting the Israelites. Jeremiah insists that there can be no quick return. He exhorts the exiles to "seek the peace and prosperity of the city to which [God has] carried you into exile" (Jer. 29:7). God's people have lived before as a minority amid other nations, and for the present they must do so again.

We do not know a great deal about the life of the Israelites while they were in exile. Certainly their situation in Babylon must have been far from pleasant—but there were worse conquerors than the Babylonians. The Israelites were at least able to be part of the Babylonian Empire while remaining in their own communities and holding on to some of their cultural and religious distinctiveness. Nevertheless, the Old Testament narratives of Daniel and Esther deal with the conflicts of loyalty that could arise for committed Israelites in exile.

The book of Daniel tells of the experiences of Daniel and three other young Israelites taken off to Babylon about fifteen years before the mass exile of 587-586 BC. Daniel's story is an amazing account of an Israelite rising to political heights in exile while refusing to compromise his faith. The four young men refuse to compromise their dietary laws and yet flourish in a place where lavish food is customary. Daniel's three friends refuse to worship the image Nebuchadnezzar sets up (Dan. 3). They survive their punishment—being thrown alive into a furnace—and afterward are promoted within the government of Babylon. Daniel also resists idolatry. He will not pray to the image of Nebuchadnezzar, and he too survives his punishment in the lions' den (Dan. 6). With God's help, Daniel (unlike Babylon's own wise men) is able to interpret Nebuchadnezzar's dreams (ch. 2, 4).

The second half of the book of Daniel contains Daniel's own symbol-filled visions that provide insight as to how history will unfold. Empires will rise and fall in turn, but their rising and falling comes in the context of the Lord's eternal reign (2:44; 4:3, 34; 6:26). Indeed, one of the great messages of Daniel is that the sovereign God honors his servants as they put God first in their lives.

Ezra and Nehemiah: Israel Returns to the Land

In 539 BC, the Persian King Cyrus defeats Babylon and allows the Israelites to return to their land. Many but by no means do all of them return. The book of Esther is set in the reign of the later Persian King Xerxes (486-465 BC) and offers another fascinating story about Israelites in exile.

Esther, an Israelite, is chosen to replace Vashti as King Xerxes' queen. Around this time the king elevates a noble called Haman to high political position. All the royal officials kneel and honor him, but Esther's cousin (and foster father) Mordecai will not do so, presumably because this is too close to idolatry. Haman is furious and obtains Xerxes' permission to have all the Israelites in the empire killed. Mordecai sends news of this threat to Esther and suggests, "Who knows but that you have come to royal position for such a time as this?" (Esth. 4:14).

To save the Jews, Esther intervenes with Xerxes by exposing Haman's plot, and Haman is hanged. Mordecai, like Joseph and Daniel, rises to great political heights. It is intriguing that the name of God is never used in the book of Esther, though she does call the people to fast—and such fasting presumably includes offering prayer to God (4:16). Yet the story exudes a powerful sense of God's providence in the experience of the Israelites who remain in exile. The festival of Purim among Jews to this day celebrates this deliverance (9:18-32).

The books of the Chronicles end on exactly the same note with which the book of Ezra begins: Cyrus, king of Persia, proclaims a decree that the temple shall be rebuilt in Jerusalem (538 BC). This offers great hope, for it is the Lord who has moved Cyrus's heart to do this (Ezra 1:1; cf. Isa. 44:28-45:1, 13). Cyrus releases any of the exiles who desire to return in order to rebuild the temple at Jerusalem. Many, but not all, choose to do so. We can only imagine their feelings as they make their way back to the land fifty years after the temple was destroyed. Once they have settled into their towns, they gather in Jerusalem and, under the leadership of Jeshua and Zerubbabel, begin to rebuild the altar of the God of Israel. This is an act of great courage because other peoples have settled in these areas while the Israelites were in exile, and the Israelites do not know how these people will react.

As soon as the altar is rebuilt, the Israelites celebrate the Feast of Tabernacles, a reminder of the time when the Israelites lived in tents in the desert wilderness on their way to the promised land from Egypt. The altar and the worship of God serve as potent symbols of God's presence among his people in the land again. Even though the temple is not yet rebuilt, the Israelites' worship provides a great sign of hope. Once they renew the rituals of worship, they get on with rebuilding the temple. The project to rebuild the Jerusalem temple suffers from local and even international opposition, but eventually the builders prevail. With strong encouragement from the preaching of the prophets Haggai and Zechariah (Ezra 6:14), the courageous Israelite builders complete the temple and dedicate it to the Lord some twenty years after their return from exile in Babylon (516 BC).

> **The altar and the worship of God serve as potent symbols of God's presence among his people in the land again.**

The reader who has been following Israel's story up to this point might be pardoned for wondering whether the Israelites will, this time, do any better than they have done in previous attempts to be a light to the nations. The rest of the books of Ezra and Nehemiah tell of the two leaders (for whom these books are named) who come to Jerusalem and play major roles in keeping the returned exiles on track. Ezra is a priest and scribe who returns to Jerusalem some sixty years after the temple is dedicated. By this time the Israelites have begun to allow intermarriage between their own people and foreigners and thus have again opened the door to idolatry through syncretism. Ezra confesses this sin, reminding the people of God's grace in allowing his people to return to the land, and dissolves such marriages.

Nehemiah is a cupbearer in the royal court of Artaxerxes in Babylon. When he hears of the desolate state of the walls of Jerusalem, Nehemiah requests and receives permission to return to Jerusalem (around 445-444 BC). In the face of violent opposition, Nehemiah leads the effort to rebuild the walls of the city (Neh. 1-7). Ezra gathers the Israelites and reads to them from the law of Moses, and the Levites instruct them in the law (Neh. 8). The people weep from a deep sense of their sin as they hear the law. Later the Levites lead them in prayer as they review their relationship with God, from creation through the call of Abraham and on to the present. They pray fervently to God and renew the covenant between the Lord and the nation of Israel (9:38-10:39).

At the end of the Old Testament, Israel's future remains uncertain. Israelites are back in the land, but even with the temple rebuilt their existence as a nation is tenuous. The temple itself has nothing like its former glory (cf. Hag. 2:3). If we focus just on Israel's political situation at this point in its history, we might have real doubts about its future. But the prophets give us a much stronger assurance about the future of Israel and about the triumph of God's purposes for the people. Although much of the prophets' preaching relates directly to the immediate situation of Israel, they also look toward the future of the nation and speak of what is to come. They use imagery culled from the history of Israel, speaking of the future of the "son of David," of "Mount Zion," of Israel as God's servant, and of the temple, and evoking for the Israelites a vision of what is to come.

To a great extent the message of the prophets is that God is going to judge people because of their continued disobedience. God's own reputation among the nations of the world is at stake in Israel's life as God's people, and thus God cannot forever tolerate Israel's rebellion. This naturally raises questions concerning God's purposes for the future—both for Israel itself and for the whole creation. Even as the prophets pronounce present judgment on Israel, they also look to the future and declare that God's purposes will triumph. Isaiah envisions a "shoot from the stump of Jesse" who will bring justice and righteousness and

> God's own reputation among the nations of the world is at stake in Israel's life as God's people, and thus God cannot forever tolerate Israel's rebellion.

usher in a time in which "the wolf will live with the lamb . . . and a little child shall lead them" (11:1-9). He predicts the coming of a suffering servant who will truly be a light to the nations (49:6; 52:13-53:12). Jeremiah 31 speaks of a "new covenant" and Ezekiel 40-48 of a "new temple." All the prophets, in one way or another, envision a future of peace between God and creation.

Together these images evoke a vision of a time when God will act decisively to establish his purposes in creation and among his people. The Messiah, the anointed one, David's true Son, will come, and Israel will be genuinely converted. The hearts of the people will turn at last to God (as in Micah 5). During this time the nations, especially all those who have opposed the Lord, will endure God's judgment. But it will also be a time of salvation for the nations.

God keeps promises. God will renew Israel and then draw all nations to himself, just as he promised Abraham. In that process the whole of the creation is to be renewed. God's kingdom will be established over the whole earth. On this profound note of hope the Old Testament ends.

Reflections for Today

In Act 3, Scene 1, of the biblical drama, we saw Israel called to embody God's purposes for humankind and to enjoy the blessings that flow from following God's perfect rule. In Scene 2, Israel is given the homeland in which this new life of blessing is meant to unfold. It's as if in Scene 1, God had selected the cast (Israel) and given them their lines (the law). Now, in Scene 2, they're on the world stage. The script couldn't be better, and the Director is there to help at every turn of the action. All the same their performance is a disaster. Why?

Let's look back briefly at what we have seen in this chapter, beginning with the book of Joshua. God is faithful to his people, giving them the land he had promised and going before them to drive out the enemy. But Israel's loyalty is divided: she tolerates the worship of idols. By the end of the book of Judges, God's chosen people have fallen so far that it is hard to tell them apart from the pagan nations that surround them. In the books of Samuel, God again acts in mercy, giving the people a king to rekindle Israel's devotion to God and allowing the nation to shine like a beacon in the darkness. But Israel's kings too often succumb to their own sinfulness, leading their people not in devotion to God but in rebellion by tolerating—and often actively encouraging—the worship of false gods. This continues to the point at which Israel's witness to the Creator's presence in its own world has been virtually extinguished. In judgment, God removes the people from their home, sending them into exile and prematurely bringing down the curtain on their performance.

Though there are many lessons for us in this part of the biblical drama, perhaps the most compelling, and the one we most need to understand in our own day, is that the worship of idols brings ruin. We were created to worship God alone. Looking back at Israel's fascination with the idols of the pagan cultures surrounding them we wonder how they could have been so foolish. They had the living God, the Creator of heaven and earth, who had miraculously led them out of slavery across a sea and a desert and a river. God had broken down fortresses in front of their eyes and given them a wonderful home. But they preferred to worship bits of stone and wood and bronze, the "gods" that had been worshiped in that part of the world long before Israel arrived there.

Those particular idols are not seductive to us. Yet many idols continue to shape human life in Western culture. When a cultural community centers its life in some part of creation and trusts that to bring life, there is idolatry. For Israel, living in an agrarian economy, the idol was agricultural fruitfulness and abundance. Today we have different idols. We have trusted in human ability to shape our own fate and deal with the problems of the world. We have trusted our reason, especially as it finds expression in science, to give us the truths we need to guide our lives. This is especially clear in the way we have trusted the social sciences to give us the pattern of the ideal society. We have trusted in human reason, science, and technology to solve our problems and progress toward a better world and a prosperous life. Yet idolatry brings death. In the words of the prophet Ezekiel to Israel: "You will suffer the penalty . . . and bear the consequences of your sins of idolatry" (23:49). This is the message of Act 3, Scene 2, but also of our culture today.[1]

Idolatry may come at a communal and cultural level. It may also take different personal forms. Whenever we center our personal lives around some part of creation rather than the God we were made to serve, there is idolatry. Pleasure, material possessions, social status, leisure—all good gifts in themselves and part of God's

> Pleasure, material possessions, social status, leisure—all good gifts in themselves and part of God's blessing on our lives—can easily become objects of our service.

blessing on our lives—can easily become objects of our service. We can see the fruits of such idolatry in the growing gap between the rich and the poor, in our frantic scramble to pile up more and more money and things at the expense of our families and our own health, in political and military conflicts around the globe born of selfishness, envy, fear, and greed. In our day, as in the days of the patriarchs and prophets, those who seek to live faithfully out of the biblical story must oppose the idolatry that characterizes the surrounding culture and "keep . . . from idols" (1 John 5:21).

Yet there is good news: God's answer to idolatry is a faithful King. Israel's kings were mostly men whose hearts proved as idolatrous as the people they ruled. However, Jesus is the King who fulfills the promise made to David. He carries out his ministry faithfully and embodies the meaning of the temple in his work, taking on himself, as the Lamb of God, the sin of the world. He defeats the enemies of God's people at the cross and writes God's law on his people by his Spirit. Jesus, son of David, Son of God, leads us out of idolatry into a new and redeemed human life, inaugurating a kingdom that brings renewal and peace to the whole creation.

Finding Our Place in the Story

1. We have seen how ancient Israel often abandoned God and turned to idols. What forms of idolatry still lure Christians and the Church?

2. We have seen that the people of ancient Israel often took their relationship with God for granted, forgetting that God's blessings would come to them only as they remained faithful and obedient partners in the covenant (Deut. 30:11-20). How do we sometimes take our relationship with God for granted? What is the basis of our own covenant with God?

3. The Old Testament prophets warned about where unfaithfulness would lead the people, and also gave hope to those who were trying to live faithfully. How are these messages of hope and of warning still relevant to us today?

4. We no longer live in a semi-theocratic regime like Israel. How do God's laws inform public life in Western democracies such as ours?

5. In what ways do you think God's judgments still operate in our time? Is it possible to clearly identify them?

Interlude

A Kingdom Story Waiting for an Ending—The Intertestamental Period

A s the Old Testament portion of the story drew to a close, the people of Israel were living on the land in relative peace under the rule of the Persians. But four hundred years later, as the New Testament story begins, Israel is living in a very different world under the brutal mastery of imperial Rome. This new situation forms the context of the New Testament. In our journey through the biblical story, we must therefore pause to consider the intertestamental period: Israel's history in the period between the end of Malachi and the beginning of Matthew that the Bible does not cover.

The Jewish Community in Palestine and the Diaspora

Though the Persian conquerors had permitted the Jews to return to their own land from exile in Babylon, only a minority of them did so. Those who did return to Palestine managed to reestablish a thriving Jewish community there, and it is this community that we often read about in the pages of the Gospels. But most Jewish people remained outside their homeland in many cities of the Roman Empire. These are called the *diaspora,* which means "scattered." Diaspora Jews maintained their distinctive covenant identity by establishing synagogues for Sabbath worship, prayer, and study of the Torah. They oriented their lives to the temple and kept their faith and hope alive with important Jewish festivals.

Israel's Faith

Five fundamental beliefs, the product of Israel's journey with God from the time of Abraham, shaped Jewish life during the intertestamental period:

- Monotheism: Israel believed in one God, the Creator of the world and Ruler of history.
- Election: God had chosen Israel for a special purpose; through this nation God would work to rid the creation of evil.
- Torah: God had given Israel the law to direct its way of life as God's holy people and promised that the Israelites would be blessed if they continued in steadfast faithfulness to this law.
- Land and temple: The land, and particularly the temple, was holy because it was here that God dwelt with Israel (Zech. 2:12). Thus the Jews believed themselves to have been chosen to serve and worship the one true God in the temple at Jerusalem and to experience God's blessing as they lived under the direction of God's word. As a faithful priestly kingdom, they were to share these blessings with the surrounding nations. But their own unfaithfulness had kept them from receiving what God had promised.
- Hope for a future redemptive act of God: Though Israel would be punished for its sin, through the prophets God promised to restore to Israel what he had always intended for them.

Growing Tension: From Persia to Rome

These fundamental beliefs were severely tested by Israel's actual experience during the four hundred years between the testaments. Though the people had in part returned to the land promised them by God, even those now in Palestine remained under the domination of one foreign power after another, almost as if their exile had never ended. They must have asked many times what had become of the promises of the prophets.

Life within the Persian Empire

When the Persian King Cyrus had ordered, as long ago as the sixth century BC, that the Jews should be allowed to return to their homeland, they must have felt a tremendous sense of elation. Surely this was the deliverance God had promised. But elation soon gave way to discouragement. The experience of the returning exiles did not measure up to what they had expected. First, not all of them returned to the land: many remained where they had settled. And although the temple had been rebuilt, the new temple seemed to them a shabby thing compared to the glorious temple of Solomon's day (Hag. 2:3). Though the Israelites were allowed once again to settle in Palestine, they remained there only at the pleasure of their foreign (and thus pagan) rulers.

Israel had been physically restored to its land, yet politically and religiously it remained a nation in exile. Why should this be? This urgent question haunted the Jews. Some reasoned that God had not yet finished judging the people for violating the covenant; they could expect a full and final deliverance only when they demonstrated a sufficient measure of faithfulness to the Torah. As a result of this belief, an oral tradition of teaching sprang up in which scholars sought to apply the ancient laws of the Torah to the new situations in which the people found themselves, in an effort to prove their faithfulness. In addition, the Jews established synagogues for teaching God's law to the common people.

> Israel had been physically restored to its land, yet politically and religiously it remained a nation in exile.

The Greek Empire under Alexander the Great

When (in 331 BC) Alexander's armies conquered the Persians, the control of Palestine fell to the Greeks. Yet the more serious threat to Israel's existence was neither military nor political but cultural. Alexander's vision was to consolidate his new empire by imposing Greek culture, including the Greek language. Although Alexander did not force the Jews to conform, Greek ideas and practices began to saturate Israel's culture. These influences, coupled with the pervasive use of the Greek language, became so influential that Jewish scholars even translated their sacred Scriptures into Greek (the Septuagint). All of this began to undermine Israel's religious integrity as the people of God. This pressure to conform to pagan cultural patterns would only intensify in the years to come.

The Greek Empire after Alexander

When Alexander died with no heir at the age of only thirty-three (in 323 BC), a struggle ensued among his generals for his massive empire. Two dynasties—the Ptolemies in Egypt and the Seleucids in Syria—ruled their respective fragments of Alexander's former empire and fought each other's armies for overall mastery of the area around Palestine. Caught between these two bitter rivals, Israel was ruled first by the Ptolemaic faction (311-198 BC) and then by the Seleucids (198-164 BC). In the latter period, the tension between Israel's faith in God's promises and its experience of life in the midst of an alien culture came to a dramatic crisis during the reign of King Antiochus IV Epiphanes.

Antiochus faced two grave threats to his empire, one external and one internal. Rome, a growing world power, was demanding large sums from Antiochus as "tribute," and the ethnic diversity of the Greek Empire itself threatened to tear it apart from within. Antiochus answered these threats first by invading various client states and looting them to pay his debts, and second by attempting to homogenize the empire by forcing his subject peoples to adopt Greek culture wholesale.

Both of these policies were perceived by many in Israel as direct assaults on the nation's life as the covenant people of God. In his ruthless attempt to make the Jews adopt Greek culture, Antiochus passed strict laws against all of the religious practices that marked Israel as God's own people. He forbade circumcision, the observance of the Sabbath, and temple sacrifices. Those who dared to disobey were put to death by cruel means. Copies of the Torah were burned and Jews were ordered to offer unclean sacrifices to pagan gods. Finally, on December 25, 167 BC, Antiochus desecrated the temple, setting up an altar within it to Zeus, the preeminent god of the Greek pantheon, and offering a pig—the most unclean animal in Jewish law—as a sacrifice. Outraged Jews referred to this act as "the abomination that causes desolation" (Dan. 11:31).

But Antiochus had not reckoned with the Jews' tenacious faith in God and their commitment to him. They believed that the Lord would act to vindicate his name, and so they rose up against their Seleucid overlords.

The Maccabean Revolt and Hasmonean Dynasty (167-163 BC)

It all began with an elderly priest, Mattathias ben Johanan, who refused to offer up an unclean sacrifice to one of the pagan gods. He killed both the compromising Jew who did offer the sacrifice and the attending Greek soldier. After this act of defiance, Mattathias fled to the desert with his five sons and there organized a band of rebels into an insurgency. When the old priest died the next year, his third son, Judah, assumed leadership of these guerrilla warriors. Judah was nicknamed Maccabee, "the hammer," and so the rebels loyal to him came to be called Maccabeans.

Though hopelessly outnumbered by the opposing Seleucid army, the Maccabeans achieved many remarkable victories. On December 25, 164 BC, three years to the day after Antiochus's desecration of the temple, Judah Maccabee (also known by the Latinate form of his name, Judas Maccabaeus) rode into Jerusalem to shouts of "hosanna" and the waving of palm branches. He cleansed the temple, removing from it the images of Greek gods, the foreign altars, and the other despised trappings of pagan worship, and rededicated the temple to the Lord. A new feast, Hanukkah, was established to memorialize this remarkable deliverance (1 Macc. 4:41-61). Twenty years later Seleucid rule was completely removed from Israel (142 BC). This ushered in a period of Jewish independence and self-rule, during which the descendants of Judah Maccabee's older brother Simon (the Hasmoneans) governed for eighty years.

It's important to know about these events in order to understand the ongoing story of Israel. Like the exodus, these events became a defining moment in Jewish history. God had acted to deliver the Israelites, to restore the temple, and to vindicate the law. And since God had visited the Israelites once in this dramatic act of redemption, surely God would do so again. But it was not to be—not yet. Although the rebel leaders Mattathias ben Johanan and his famous son Judah Maccabee were committed to God's law, the Hasmonean kings that followed were deeply compromised by pagan Greek culture and by their concern to maintain their political power.

Israel within the Fist of Rome

Meanwhile Rome had been rising steadily in power. In the early years of the first century BC, Rome became the dominant military and political force in its part of the world. In 63 BC Pompey the Great marched into Jerusalem to bring Israel within the Roman Empire, beginning a Roman presence there that was to last nearly five hundred years. Rome chose to rule Israel indirectly through cooperative (and thus compromising) puppet kings and governors: these included the last of the Hasmoneans, Herod the Great (and his descendants), and finally a series of Roman-appointed procurators, including Pontius Pilate.

The frustration and anger that Israel had always felt for its pagan masters now found a new target in Rome, the most powerful and brutal of them all. Many who looked to the Scriptures for understanding now identified Rome with the vicious beast of Daniel (Dan. 7:7). The Romans ruled the Jews by force, fear, and intimidation, trampling on their religious sensitivities, taxing them into poverty, enforcing their own brand of pagan culture, and meting out savage punishments for any who opposed their will.

Under this oppressive regime, racial hatred of Gentiles increased in Israel. It spilled over to include hatred against any of the Jews who collaborated with Rome, including many of the priests and tax collectors, as well as the Roman-appointed King Herod and his cronies. The common people's longing for God's intervention grew stronger and stronger. From time to time this zeal for a new kingdom to be ruled by God broke out into local acts of armed rebellion against the hated Roman usurpers. These were swiftly and violently put down, ending with mass crucifixions of the would-be rebels, a grisly exhibition of the price to be paid for opposing Rome.

Still, Israel remained a stubborn and intransigent province of the empire for almost a century before the birth of Jesus and for a century after. During this period about ten or twelve revolutionary movements arose around some self-designated messianic leader. So the Israel in which Jesus was born was a nation in which hope for God's kingdom was intense, even feverish. And they were ready to act to help usher it in.

> The Israel in which Jesus was born was a nation in which hope for God's kingdom was intense, even feverish.

Israel's Hope for the Kingdom

The people of Israel thought of history as having two very distinct periods: the present age and the age to come. In the present age, which had begun with Adam's rebellion against God's rule, the whole of creation had been stained by sin and evil. But in the age to come God would intervene to cleanse and renew the creation. This renewal would begin with Israel; they would be a forgiven, cleansed, and renewed people. Through this nation, newly prepared for its task, God would extend the blessings of restoration to the surrounding Gentile nations and even to the creation itself. All of this would take place in the last days of history: God's Spirit would be poured out and the present evil age would draw to a close. God would act in power to save the creation from the ravages of sin, Satan, pain, and death.

This division of history into two eras was rooted in the writings of the Old Testament prophets. In the last days of history God would visit the earth to restore his cosmic rule and bring about a comprehensive salvation from evil, in which the knowledge of God and justice and peace would fill the earth. This salvation would begin with Israel, and then all the nations would be gathered to Israel.

Some Jews believed that the Gentile nations would finally acknowledge Israel's God as their own King and joyfully live under his rule (Isa. 49:6); the nations would flock to Zion to learn the way of God (Isa. 2:3). But many more inclined to a different prophetic theme in Scripture. Israel's long years of humiliation had bred such hatred for the pagan oppressors that the Israelites looked for the nations to be dashed into pieces like pottery (Ps. 2:9). They believed God would deliver them in violent judgment.

This mighty act of deliverance would be accomplished by a *messiah* (the Hebrew word meaning "anointed"). They expected an anointed king or priest to be the divine agent of redemption who would usher in God's renewed kingdom. There were many conflicting notions of what kind of Messiah the nation should expect to see when God at last sent a messenger to deliver them: a royal or priestly Messiah or one or more Messiahs, human or divine. But any notion of a suffering Messiah was almost entirely absent (cf. Luke 24:25).

The image that best captured Israel's expectation was "the kingdom of God." Israel looked to a day when there would be "no king but God." God would return to the temple and would once again come to dwell among the people (Mal. 3:1). The nation would be liberated from its bondage to pagan oppressors. The Messiah would sweep away the rule of Caesar and of his puppet kings and priests in Israel and set things right under God's rule. God

> The image that best captured Israel's expectation was "the kingdom of God."

would pour his Spirit on the people, who would be renewed in obedience and faithfulness toward God. Jews of past generations who had remained faithful to God would be raised from the dead (Dan. 12:2).

Until that day, the faithful in Israel lived in hope: they prayed, studied the Scriptures, celebrated the festivals, remained faithful to the Torah, and continued to be ready for military action. On this scenario, most agreed. But on the matters of how, when, and through whom God would accomplish these things, and concerning how they were to live until that day, the Jews were often bitterly divided.

Differing Expressions of Israel's Hope

The Pharisees

One expression of this hope was found in a prominent group called the Pharisees. The Pharisees were concerned about Jewish compromise to Greek culture; they believed God could not act to bring the kingdom if Israel remained polluted. To combat this compromise, they called for an urgent commitment to two things: complete separation from pagan corruption and radical obedience to the Torah. To the Pharisees, separation and obedience were two sides of one essential truth. They emphasized the aspects of Torah law that marked the Jewish people as unique. So circumcision, food laws, and observing the Sabbath assumed new significance as boundary markers that divided faithful Jews from faithless pagans. The Pharisees operated primarily in the synagogues as teachers of the law and the oral tradition.

Many Pharisees were also ready to advance this revolution with political activism and even with violence. Their popularity and success derived mainly from giving voice to some of the deepest desires of the people of Israel: their longing for liberation, their loyalty to the Torah, and their long-held hope for a renewed kingdom in which God himself would reign over his people.

The Essenes

This group also arose during the Maccabean revolt and was driven by the same desire to reverse the assimilation into Greek culture that continued to plague Israel. But unlike the Pharisees, they were not content to work within the system. The Essenes chose the path of withdrawal. Since they believed that the corruption of Greek culture had become deeply rooted in Israel, the Essenes turned their backs on all of it. They believed that they alone were the true Israel. Many withdrew to form an alternative community in the desert outside Jericho where they studied the Scriptures, prayed, and enforced careful adherence to the Torah. They believed that their faithfulness to the Torah would bring God back to restore the fortunes of Israel.

The Sadducees and Priests

These were the official teachers of the law and the recognized representatives of mainline Jewish religion. Along with the Pharisees they were members of the ruling council, the Sanhedrin. Because they depended on the favor of the Romans for their influential positions in society, the priests and Sadducees certainly did not have the revolutionary spirit of the Pharisees or the Essenes. They maintained their power by collaborating with the Romans, and so they had every reason to maintain the status quo.

The Zealots

The Zealots were a very loosely organized group, drawing people from different levels of Israel's society, including many Pharisees. They took their inspiration from the account of the old priest Mattathias, initiator of the Maccabean revolt. He rallied support by crying out, "Let every one who is zealous for the law and supports the covenant come out with me!" (1 Macc. 2:27, NRSV). The Zealots carried on this tradition: they were loyal to the Torah, fiercely resisted compromise with pagan culture, embraced the use of violence to achieve their ends, and were willing to be martyred for the cause.

By the time of Jesus many groups of Zealots in Israel were eager to participate in armed revolt to liberate their people and cleanse the land and temple of pagan pollution. Often these bands of revolutionaries were led by a self-proclaimed Messiah. Inevitably, the Roman authorities would crush such rebels, crucify the "Messiah," and savagely punish his followers (cf. Acts 5:36-37). Scripture identifies one of Jesus' own apostles as Simon the Zealot (Luke 6:15), and perhaps Peter and other disciples were Zealots too.

The Common People

Most of the Jews of this period were not members of any party. The faithful among them looked for a day when God would return to redeem them from their pagan oppressors. They would then be free to obey the Torah and to worship God in a cleansed temple on a cleansed land. The promised Messiah was the focus of their longing, and until his coming, they sought to be faithful so that God would speed the day. They attempted to learn about the Torah at the synagogue and obey it as best they could. They celebrated the festivals, prayed, kept the food laws and the Sabbath, and circumcised their baby boys. And they waited in hope.

Into this cauldron of swirling factions, insurgencies, compromises, and fervent expectations, a young man from Nazareth, the son of a carpenter, came to announce that the kingdom of God had come to Israel and was even now present in him.

Reflections for Today

As we look for connections between the intertestamental period and our own day, let's reflect for a moment on three of these very different groups within Israel and their distinctive approaches to living a life of faith in the midst of an alien and pagan culture. Their names may seem bizarre to modern ears but their methods look suspiciously like some familiar features on the twenty-first century religious landscape.

First, the Zealots. They attempted to root out paganism from among them by using sabotage, arson, and even murder to harass the occupying Greeks and Romans. We might compare them to some militants of our own day who express what they would describe as their devotion to God in acts of public protest, in marches and rallies—and sometimes in criminal violence. Some of these modern-day zealots have in the most extreme cases chosen the sinful methods of those whom they see as their enemies, until it is hard to distinguish one from the other: consider the anti-abortionist, motivated by a determination to preserve life, whose tactics include the murder of doctors and the bombing of clinics—and thus the willful destruction of human life.

Simon, one of Jesus' own disciples (not the one later called Peter), had once been a Zealot. I wonder how difficult it was for Simon to really hear Jesus when

> **Jesus was describing a way to fight back against injustice with the powerful weapon of sacrificial love.**

he said, "Love your enemies, do good to those who hate you, bless those who curse you, pray for those who mistreat you. If someone slaps you on one cheek, turn the other also. If someone takes your cloak, do not withhold your shirt. Give to everyone who asks you, and if anyone takes what belongs to you, do not demand it back. Do to others as you would have them do to you" (Luke 6:27-31).

Jesus was describing a way to fight back against injustice with the powerful weapon of sacrificial love—and there is no more eloquent expression of that love than Jesus' own death for the sake of his enemies. Who are the zealots among us today?

Second, the Essenes, whose tactic was to withdraw completely from the surrounding "pagan" culture and to establish their own completely separate and "holy" community. We might think here of the monasteries and convents in which, historically, some members of the Church have sought to separate themselves from the world and devote themselves wholly to prayer. But withdrawal of a different sort is practised by many Christians today who would not dream of entering a monastery! These modern-day Essenes often seek to shut themselves off in a cultural cocoon of exclusively "Christian" books, conversation, music, television, films, friends, and even vacations. Their withdrawal and lack of understanding of the world around them may seem like a positive virtue. But like the Essenes of the intertestamental period, these Christians neglect one of the most significant elements of God's covenant with his people. We are called to be active in the world, a welcoming community, a people whose lives so openly reflect the goodness and grace of God that those around us will be eager to join the fellowship of God. Discerning how to live in the midst of a secular human culture is always a risky undertaking, and it may seem simpler to pull away from it all. But God calls us to be engaged in the ongoing work of redeeming the world.

Third, the Sadducees, who survived by compromising with the Greeks and Romans, some of them even accepting positions of authority within the hated governments of occupation. They could negotiate this kind of life by keeping their heads down, keeping what faith they had to themselves, and trying above all to fit in. Perhaps one of them might privately feel a measure of contempt for the pagan who worked next to him—but he would be highly unlikely to reveal such feelings, much less to try to influence his foreign neighbour. Keeping one's religious convictions strictly separate from one's daily life is the hallmark of a Sadducee.

This is the life of a chameleon, and for many modern Christians it is the most tempting option of the three, for it seems so safe to be invisible. But this is surely not what God intended for the people who were meant to show the world the richness and glory of a life lived according to God's Word: "You are the light of the world. A city on a hill cannot be hidden. Neither do people light a lamp and put it under a bowl. Instead they put it on its stand, and it gives light to everyone in the house. In the same way, let your light shine before others, that they may see your good deeds and praise your Father in heaven" (Matt. 5:14-16). Notice that Jesus says that the lives of his followers are to be attractive—their "good deeds" should be evident to all—but that it is the Father who is glorified.

Finding Our Place in the Story

1. In the time between the testaments, many Israelites either "sold out" to the surrounding pagan culture or reacted against it in hatred, withdrawing and isolating themselves. How are these two dangers still present in the Church?

2. What attitude should Christians have toward the (predominantly pagan) cultures in which they live? How does Jesus' example show us the way?

3. We have seen what a powerful force hope was in the intertestamental period. Where does modern Western culture place its hope for the future? What is the basis of our hope and how can it shape our lives?

Act 4

The Coming of the King— Redemption Accomplished

We cannot grasp the meaning of the story of Jesus until we begin to see that it is in fact the climactic episode of the great drama of the Bible, the true story of the whole world.

Jewish Expectation for God's Kingdom

Jesus' entire mission turns on the central theme of the kingdom of God. He proclaims this in his first words in Mark's Gospel: "The time has come. . . . The kingdom of God has come near. Repent and believe the good news!" (Mark 1:15). But then Jesus goes further: not only has God's kingdom come at last to Israel, it has come in himself! (Luke 4:18, 21). He, Jesus of Nazareth, has been sent by the Father for one purpose alone: to make known the good news of the kingdom (4:43).

Jesus does not bother to define or explain the phrase "the kingdom of God." Those to whom he is speaking are quite familiar with such language. After all, there is a widespread expectation among the Jews of first-century Palestine and of the diaspora that God is about to act—soon, suddenly, in love and wrath and power—to renew creation and restore his reign over the whole world. But until God acts, how should one live in anticipation of that day?

In the preceding "Interlude" of our drama we surveyed four well-known answers to these questions: the Pharisees taught religious separation, the Essenes advocated withdrawal, the Zealots espoused violent revolution, and the Sadducees promoted political compromise with the Roman authorities. Four very different approaches—yet bound together by a common loathing for Gentiles. And then comes Jesus, who refuses to walk any of these paths. He moves in a startlingly different way: it is the way of love and of suffering, "love of enemies instead of their destruction; unconditional forgiveness instead of retaliation; readiness to suffer instead of using force; blessing for peacemakers instead of hymns of hate and revenge."[1]

Jesus Prepares for his Kingdom Mission

The Bible declares that the birth of Jesus is the incarnation—literally, "making in flesh"—of God in human history. As happens so often in the drama of God's redemption, this story begins with a miraculous birth. Jesus is begotten not by his earthly father, Joseph, but by the power of the Holy Spirit who causes the virgin Mary to become pregnant (Matt. 1:18-23; Luke 1:26-35). His birth announcement is made to outcast shepherds: "I bring you good news of great joy! This is good news for all people! Today a Savior-King has been born. He is the long-awaited Messiah, the Lord!" (Luke 2:10-11; our paraphrase). Jesus grows up in Nazareth with his brothers and sisters, the son of a carpenter. Little is known of these years except that his awareness of his sonship to God (whom he calls "Father") and his mission is already beginning to develop (2:41-50).

Jesus' public mission begins in connection with his cousin John the Baptist (Mark 1:1-8), who has appeared in Palestine with a message from God. John's message: The kingdom is about to come. God is about to act, to rule people just as the Old Testament prophets promised. God's kingdom will be inaugurated by the "Coming One" who brings salvation and judgment. The kingdom of God is so close, John says, that the winnowing fork separating (godly) wheat from (ungodly) chaff is already in the hand of the Messiah (Luke 3:9, 17). John's own task—just as Isaiah promised—is to prepare the way for the coming King; to prepare the people to receive him (Isa. 40:3-5; cf. Mal. 3:1; 4:5-6).

John's message is that the King's subjects must repent—turn from sin to God, seeking the promised salvation—and be baptized in water. Even the location is important, since for the Jews geography is drenched with symbolic meaning. John baptizes in the Jordan River because it was here that, more than a thousand years earlier, Israel entered the promised land to become God's light to the nations. John's return to this place signals a new summons from God to Israel to carry out that original—and long-neglected—task. Baptism is a vivid symbol of this new beginning, suggesting cleansing from sin. The people of God, cleansed and ready to take up their task again, symbolically cross the Jordan once more, entering into the land.

One day, among the crowds who have come to John to be baptized, we find Jesus (Mark 1:9-11). In his baptism, Jesus identifies himself with the people in their brokenness and in their call. Though he does not need to be cleansed from sin, he takes on the burden of their sinful failure and the vocation of their mission to become the channel of God's salvation to the nations (Matt. 3:14-15). While he is being baptized in water, the Spirit visibly comes to equip him for his task. The Father himself confirms Jesus' calling: "You are my Son, whom I love" (Mark 1:11). These words of the Father affirm that Jesus is Israel's anointed king, the true son of David (see Ps. 2:7), here to inaugurate the kingdom of God. The Spirit will empower him to carry out God's work of salvation.

> In his baptism, Jesus identifies himself with the people in their brokenness and in their call.

Before this work begins, the Spirit leads Jesus into the wilderness to encounter Satan (Matt. 4:1-11; Mark 1:12-13). As we read the story, we must remember the differing points of view in first-century Israel concerning how God's kingdom should come, for this is what Jesus' temptation is all about.

Satan shows Jesus three different paths he might take as the Messiah: the way of the populist, the way of the wonder-worker, and the way of the violent revolutionary. By traveling the first path and turning stones into bread, Jesus could use his power to become a populist Messiah. He could give the people what they want, putting himself forward as the leader of a popular revolution. Alternatively, Jesus could become a messianic wonder-worker by throwing himself from the temple wall and forcing God to act in a spectacular way to save him. The people would follow Jesus, compelled by miracles and wonders. Or again, Jesus could become a political Messiah in the mold of the Zealots by using violence and coercion in a militarist shortcut to the throne. But to do this would be to adopt Satan's own program of domination, to bow before him.

Jesus sees that all such paths in fact begin with Satan, and he refuses to twist his own mission to conform to popular expectations of the Messiah. Instead, he chooses the hard kingdom road God laid out long ago: the road of humble service, self-giving love, and sacrificial suffering. Empowered and led by the Holy Spirit and resolute in his sense of calling as the Messiah, Jesus is ready to begin the mission given to him by the Father.

Jesus' mission begins humbly. He moves from place to place in the northern Palestine province of Galilee, often near the city of Capernaum.

Jesus Announces the Arrival of the Kingdom

Jesus announces good news: the kingdom of God has arrived (Mark 1:14-15). The Greek word here for "good news" (*euangelion*) is the word commonly used in that culture for the kind of announcement that brings great joy. It might be news of a wedding, the birth of a son, or a military victory. Jesus announces the good news that God's power to save the creation has arrived. This is not the sort of announcement that would be tucked away in the religion section of the newspaper; this is front-page stuff: *"God is now acting in love and power through Jesus and by his Spirit to restore all of creation and all of human life to live again under the benevolent reign of God himself."*

Some messages can be received merely for information. Others— "There's a fire in the building!"— require an immediate response. We cannot remain impassive once we have heard the news that at last God's universal kingdom is coming. This message demands a response. Jesus calls those who hear him to "repent and believe," and then he says simply, "Follow me" (1:15-17).

> We cannot remain impassive once we have heard the news that at last God's universal kingdom is coming. This message demands a response.

We might paraphrase Jesus' call to repent and believe this way: "Turn from your false views of the world and embrace the reality and presence of the coming kingdom of God in me. You may not see the power of God's healing kingdom breaking into history, but you can believe that in me God's liberating power is now present. Give up your old way of life, and trust me for a new one."

Jesus then calls those who have repented and believed to follow him. In Jesus' day a disciple would give up his own plans to follow a rabbi, learning the Torah and all the rabbi's ways. Jesus gives an invitation: "Come. Be with me. Learn from me. Give up your own way of life. Do what I do. Learn to live as I do." But Jesus is much more than a rabbi: he is Lord and Christ. The lives of those who choose to hear and follow Jesus will no longer be centered in the Torah but in Jesus himself. His disciples are to give full allegiance and devotion to him; they express loyalty to God's kingdom through loyalty to Jesus.

Simon and Andrew, followed by James and John, are the first to respond to Jesus' startling call on their lives. With these few, a kingdom community begins to form (1:16-20).

Jesus Reveals the Kingdom through His Mighty Works

Jesus soon validates his claim to be the Messiah of God's kingdom by some amazing acts that reveal the saving power of God at work in him. People witness miracles of healing, demons driven out, the powers of nature subdued to Jesus' will, death itself unravelling (Mark 1:21-34, 40-45). This is clear evidence that the healing and restoring power of God's kingdom has come upon the earth, confirming Jesus' own role as God's anointed King. Later, when the Pharisees accuse Jesus of doing these things by the power of Satan, Jesus gives a searing rebuke: "If I drive out demons by the finger of God, then the kingdom of God has come upon you" (Luke 11:20).

All of Jesus' deeds of power are unmistakable evidences of God's liberating power at work through him. When Jesus heals the blind (Luke 18:35-43), the lame (Mark 2:1-12), the mute and deaf (7:31-36), and the leper (Luke 17:11-19), people see God's healing power flowing into human history to end the reign of sickness and pain. When Jesus calms the sea (Mark 4:35-41) or feeds the hungry (8:1-10), he demonstrates the power of God to restore a cursed creation. When Jesus raises Lazarus (John 11) and Jairus's daughter (Mark 5:21-43), people see the power of God conquering even death. These miracles are like windows through which we catch glimpses of a renewed cosmos, from which Satan and his demons have been cast out. Sickness and pain are to be no more, death itself will be gone forever, and the creation restored to its original beauty and harmony.

The Sources of Jesus' Power Are the Holy Spirit and Prayer

One day, following an exhausting time of healing people and driving out demons, Jesus finds a solitary place to pray very early in the morning (Mark 1:35). Jesus "often" withdraws to pray, and on occasions he prays all night (Luke 5:16; 6:12). These reports of prayer take us to the heart of Jesus' ministry and the secret of his power: an intensely intimate relationship with God as a son with his father, united in the presence and power of the Spirit.

Jesus carries out his mission in intimate communion with God, addressing him as *Abba*, "Father" (Mark 14:36; John 17:1-3). An Aramaic term, *Abba* was used to express the special intimacy that can exist between close family members. "Father" was only one of the many titles by which Israel knew God, and it was most unusual for Jews to address him in such intimate terms. So it is particularly striking that when Jesus relates to God, this most intimate language becomes the primary term of address.

The Father responds to his dearly loved Son through the powerful working of the Spirit. The kingdom comes as the Spirit works in response to Jesus' prayer. The Spirit is at work in and through Jesus from the very beginning of his life (Acts 10:38). He counters the Pharisees' suspicion that the power at work in him might be demonic: "If it is by the Spirit of God that I drive out demons, then the kingdom of God has come upon you" (Matt. 12:28). Where the Spirit of God is at work, there the kingdom of God has come. Jesus maintains intimate communion with the Father in prayer, and this unleashes the Spirit's power to heal and renew.

Jesus Arouses Opposition to His Kingdom Mission

When Jesus returns to Capernaum, some of the Jewish leaders, Pharisees and teachers of the law, join the crowd that gathers to hear him. They come from as far away as Jerusalem to check out the orthodoxy of this new "kingdom" movement (Mark 2:1-12). And what they see and hear mightily disturbs them. In a series of episodes, Mark narrates the developing clash between Jesus and these skeptical leaders concerning various traditional Jewish practices (2:13-3:6). In each encounter, Jesus challenges the status quo, announcing and embodying a radically different view of the kingdom of God than that held by the official guardians of Jewish religion.

The Jewish leaders are looking for a kingdom in which Israel will be suddenly and forcibly delivered from the control of pagan Rome. (Remember that they are separatists, self-appointed guardians of Jewish identity, which they believe is under attack, threatened by the people's assimilation to the surrounding pagan culture.) Part of their strategy to keep themselves pure involves careful attention to the central place of the temple, food laws, tithing, Sabbath-keeping, and the choice of "acceptable" mealtime companions.

Jesus boldly challenges the Pharisees' rigid views on the Sabbath and food laws (Mark 2:23-3:6). He deliberately eats and drinks with all those whom the Pharisees would exclude (2:13-17). But the greater challenge to the Pharisees and the people of Israel is what these things have come to represent: separation, hatred, and a thirst for vengeance. These things have no place within God's call for the Israelites to love their neighbors, to be the channel of God's blessing to the nations, to be a light to the world. Against the Pharisees' deeply held misunderstanding of Israel's identity and vocation, Jesus holds up Israel's missionary calling: to become a different sort of kingdom in which "enemies" become "friends" not by force of arms or any other coercion, but by loving invitation.

Jesus Gathers a New Community

Early in his Galilean ministry, Jesus begins to gather a community around him (Mark 1:16-20; 2:13-14). Matthew's Gospel, written to the Jews, especially highlights the fact that Jesus' efforts to form a community take place primarily within Israel (Matt. 10:5-6; 15:24). This only makes sense within the context of Israel's prophetic hope in the first century.

The prophets promised that Israel would one day be restored, its scattered people brought together once more under God's reign (Ezek. 37; 39:23-29). So when Jesus says he is sent to the lost sheep of Israel (Matt. 15:24), he has in mind that the end-time gathering of Israel has begun. But according to the prophets, this end-time salvation will not be limited to Israel. Israel is only the first nation to be renewed, and then the (Gentile) nations will share in its salvation (Ezek. 39:27-28; cf. 37:28). Now Jesus announces the dawning of just such a day, the beginning of a renewal for Israel that eventually will draw all nations to God.

This community begins to form as Jesus announces the good news of the kingdom and calls for repentance and faith (Mark 1:14-15). Some who hear

Jesus' claims, like Mary, Martha, and Lazarus, are called to be loyal to him while remaining in their homes and villages, living out the life of God's kingdom there. Others are called to leave everything behind and hit the road with Jesus. From this latter group, Jesus appoints twelve who spend their lives with him, and he designates them apostles (from the Greek for "one who is sent," Mark 3:13-19). These, the Twelve, whose number represents the twelve tribes of Israel, become the nucleus of the renewed nation (Luke 22:30; Rev. 21:12-14). So Jesus' choosing of the Twelve is a symbolic prophetic action by which he portrays the end-time gathering of the twelve tribes of Israel to share the salvation of the kingdom.

Some who hear Jesus' claims, like Mary, Martha, and Lazarus, are called to be loyal to him while remaining in their homes and villages, living out the life of God's kingdom there. Others are called to leave everything behind and hit the road with Jesus.

Jesus appointed the Twelve for a twofold purpose: first, "that they might be with him"; and second, "that he might send them out to preach and to have authority to drive out demons" (Mark 3:14). To "be with" Jesus means that these followers are to watch him and come to know his way of life, to listen to him and to learn about life in the kingdom. It means that they will come to know Jesus' intimate communion with the Father and to model their own lives on his life, empowered by the Spirit. They will hear Jesus proclaim the good news with his words and demonstrate it in his actions. They will see a life of love (John 15:9-13), obedience (17:4), joy (15:11), peace (14:27), justice (Luke 4:18), compassion (Matt. 9:36), gentleness and humility (11:29), and solidarity with the poor and needy (Mark 2:15-17). And they will learn to build these things into their own lives. Much of the Gospels' text is taken up with Jesus teaching his disciples what it means to live as citizens of the kingdom he is bringing (e.g., Matt. 5-7). The Twelve are also called to follow Jesus so that they can participate in his mission (Mark 6:7-13; Luke 9:1-9). For the disciples, being in community with Jesus means to live like Jesus, obey his teaching, and take active part in his mission.

Jesus Welcomes Sinners and Outcasts

Within his kingdom community, Jesus includes the poor, the sick, and the lost—all those who are marginalized within Israel. He does not entirely ignore the Pharisees and religious leaders, who often characterize him as a "friend of tax collectors and sinners" (Matt. 11:19). They are welcome if they choose to come. Likening himself to a doctor who treats the sick, not the healthy, Jesus explains why his ministry is directed primarily toward sinners, not the "righteous": he has come "to seek and to save what was lost" (Luke 19:10). Jesus warmly welcomes those shunned by Jewish society into the kingdom of God.

Some specific groups—"sinners" and the poor and sick—become special objects of Jesus' attention. By sinners Luke means those in despised occupations or with immoral lifestyles. For example, most Jews shunned their own tax collectors, who were in the pay of the hated Roman occupying forces, judging them to be traitors to their own people—and many of the tax collectors did cheat and overcharge the citizens. Jesus also welcomes prostitutes and women of questionable character (Luke 7:37-50; John 8:1-11). He says to the leaders of the Jewish people, "Truly I tell you, the tax collectors and the prostitutes are entering the kingdom of God ahead of you" (Matt. 21:31). Jesus also welcomes the poor, the beggars, the sick, and the physically handicapped into the kingdom of God—even though the Jews often interpreted poverty and sickness as signs of God's judgment against an individual's sin (see John 9:1-3).

With two kinds of actions, Jesus shows that those who had been on the margins of Jewish society are welcome in the kingdom of God. First, Jesus enjoys table fellowship with these outcasts. Meals were not casual matters in Jesus' time but complex social practices that reinforced a person's social status and place in the hierarchy. The Pharisees believed that many kinds of "sinners" and the sick and the poor should be excluded from fellowship within the community because they stood under the judgment of God (see John 9:2). In choosing to eat with these people, Jesus confirms that these so-called outcasts are not barred from the Messiah's kingdom banquet.

> **Those who had been on the margins of Jewish society are welcome in the kingdom of God.**

Second, Jesus' miracles of healing also demonstrate how he accepts the marginalized into the kingdom of God. A written fragment from an Essene community around Jesus' time shows how these strict Jews excluded many from the kingdom: "Neither the blind, nor the lame, nor the deaf, nor the dumb, nor the lepers, nor those whose flesh is blemished shall be admitted to the council of the community." The Pharisees had a similar list of excluded people. Thus when Jesus touches the blind, the deaf, the lepers and the lame, he not only heals their bodies but also restores them as persons to full membership in the kingdom community.

Jesus Explains the Kingdom with Parables

Jesus announces the arrival of the kingdom of God, demonstrates it in his actions, and gathers a kingdom community. However, this kingdom does not look at all the way the Jews expected. And Jesus himself does not fit the popular understanding of the Messiah of Old Testament prophecy. For anyone in first-century Israel who takes the claims of Jesus seriously, bewilderment reigns.

We glimpse this confusion in John the Baptist when he is in Herod's jail. John has preached that the kingdom of God is near and the final judgment is about to fall (Luke 3:9, 17)—but nothing happens in the way he expected. John wonders if he has misunderstood everything. He calls his disciples and sends them to Jesus with a question: "Are you the one who was to come, or should we expect someone else?" (7:19).

It is just this kind of confusion that Jesus addresses in the parables. His disciples struggle to understand how the promises of the prophets are being fulfilled in Jesus. It certainly doesn't look the way they expect. Jesus teaches in parables to explain the nature of the kingdom that has appeared among them in such an utterly unexpected way (Matt. 13:11).

These parables are often are introduced with "The kingdom of God is like . . ." (Mark 4) or "The kingdom of heaven is like . . ." (Matt. 13). The meaning of these phrases is the same. In this series of parables, we learn the secrets of the kingdom.

The kingdom does not come all at once. Though the Jews have expected the kingdom to arrive in fullness immediately, or at least very soon after the Messiah appears, this does not happen. Sometimes Jesus talks about the kingdom as

> **Sometimes Jesus talks about the kingdom as if it is present already; other times he suggests that it is coming in the future.**

if it is present already; other times he suggests that it is coming in the future. Many of his parables help to explain this seeming contradiction. The parable of the sower and weeds teaches that in the present the kingdom comes by the "sowing" of the gospel. In the future, the sown seeds will grow up into mature plants and the weeds will be separated from the wheat (Matt. 13:24-30, 36-43; cf. 13:31-33, 47-50).

Thus the kingdom Jesus describes is both present and future: already begun, but not yet here in fullness. But how can something as important as God's kingdom have these two apparently opposite qualities? The parable of the weeds teaches that the power of evil continues alongside the new healing power that has come into the world in Jesus. The age to come overlaps with the old age; the powers of both are present.

In the present, the kingdom does not come with irresistible power. The Jews expect that when God's kingdom arrives, no enemy will be able to resist it. They remember Daniel's words: "The God of heaven will set up a kingdom. . . . It will crush all those kingdoms and bring them to an end, but it will itself endure forever" (Dan. 2:44). Who can stand against the power of God?

But Jesus says, "Listen! A farmer went out to sow his seed" (Mark 4:3)—and what a different picture emerges from his story! (See 4:1-20; Matt. 13:1-23.) The Messiah does not come as a military conqueror but as a humble farmer. The kingdom does not arrive in irresistible power and force but by the message of the kingdom. Some people receive the word, and God's power brings about the fruit of the kingdom, but others reject that message—and seem to suffer no harm.

The final judgment of the kingdom is reserved for the future. Jesus' hearers expect God's judgment to fall swiftly on the ungodly. But the parable of the weeds (Matt. 13:24-30, 36-43) shows that the judgment they expect will not fall immediately. At the end of the age judgment will indeed come; until then the powers of God's kingdom and of evil must continue together.

Many other parables similarly illustrate judgment postponed (Matt. 13:47-50; 25:1-46). When Jesus speaks of the final coming of the kingdom in his parables, he stresses readiness and faithfulness in the present. We are to respond to the message of the kingdom and live a life centered in Jesus until the last day.

The full arrival of the kingdom is postponed to allow many to enter it during the present age. Since the coming of the kingdom has already begun in Jesus, why does God not complete his work? One of Luke's parables suggests an answer (Luke 14:15-24). A banquet is made ready: the table is set and laden with food and drink. But there the host pauses; the guests must wait yet a little while. The delay gives an opportunity for the lost to also be brought in to share at the banquet table. All—and especially the poor, the lost, the forgotten ones— are invited and welcome to share in the banquet that is God's kingdom. When the Pharisees mutter that Jesus is welcoming all the wrong people, he tells them three parables: a lost sheep (Luke 15:3-7), a lost coin (15:8-10), and a lost son (15:11-32). When the lost son, who has for a time wandered from his home and family, repents and turns back, the father welcomes him with joy and favor.

Jesus tells many parables—at least forty—and we have looked at only a sampling. Yet in these few the main themes of Jesus' teaching are evident: the parables reveal the true nature of God's kingdom in contrast to the misunderstandings of Jesus' hearers.

Jesus Journeys Outside Galilee

The first part of Jesus' kingdom mission has taken place in the Galilean region surrounding Capernaum. Now, after some two years, Jesus journeys outside Galilee into Gentile territory. As opposition grows, Jesus turns his attention to instructing his disciples, preparing them to carry on his work.

Who Is Jesus?

After Jesus has been engaging in his kingdom mission for some time, there are many different opinions about him among the people. Who is this Jesus? At one point, pausing in his travels at Caesarea Philippi, Jesus confronts his disciples with the question "Who do people say I am?" They reply: "Some say John the Baptist; others say Elijah; and still others, one of the prophets." Then Jesus makes it personal: "But what about you? Who do you say I am?" On behalf of all of them, Peter answers, "You are the Messiah" (Mark 8:27-29). This—the identity of Jesus—is the heart of the matter.

The Hebrew word *messiah* (Greek: *christos*) means "anointed one." During the intertestamental period, the term "Messiah" or "Christ" was used prophetically as the title of the person (or persons) whom God would appoint to restore his rule and usher in his kingdom. The title usually took on political and military connotations. Jesus accepts the confession of Peter: indeed, Jesus is the Messiah. But he does not accept the popular understanding of who the "anointed one" is, and of what God calls him to do. Therefore Jesus warns the disciples not to tell anyone who he is (Mark 8:30). The people's expectations must be adjusted to fit the reality of Jesus. Thus though most Jews expect that the Christ will be God's agent to usher in the kingdom of God, they cannot accept his having to suffer the humiliation of crucifixion (cf. 8:31). Jesus breaks the mold of their expectations. He is God's chosen one, appointed to usher in God's kingdom—but he is also the crucified victim.

> **Jesus is God's chosen one, appointed to usher in God's kingdom—but he is also the crucified victim.**

Peter and the disciples do not yet understand this, and their misunderstanding becomes clear in the next verses. When Jesus tells them plainly that he will soon be crucified, Peter begins to argue, saying that he must be mistaken—the Christ cannot die such a shameful death (8:32). Jesus silences Peter, rebuking him sternly: Jesus must die (8:33). It takes some time before Peter himself comes to realize the full significance of his own confession that Jesus is Messiah!

To Mark's account of Peter's confession, "You are the Messiah," Matthew adds an important phrase: "the Son of the living God" (Matt. 16:16). The title "Son of God," especially given to Israel's kings, suggests a special relationship to God and a special task to fulfill in obedience to God. The Jews of Jesus' time looked for a Messiah who would be indeed a "son of God" like the Old Testament kings, especially David (2 Sam. 7:14; Ps. 2). Jesus does come to them as one who stands in just such a special relationship to God and with just such a divine task: to inaugurate God's rule. However, Jesus is more than these things. His intimacy with the Father and his messianic task are unique and exclusive. Though Jesus stands within a long tradition of "God's sons," he is in another sense absolutely unique, God's "one and only Son" (John 3:16).

The next verses in Mark give us one more important title that underscores Peter's confession. Jesus begins to teach his disciples that the "Son of Man" must suffer, die, and rise again. But who is the "Son of Man"? The title comes from Daniel 7:13-14, a text very popular in Jesus' time because of its promise of a golden future for Israel. In Jesus' time, many Jews saw Daniel's vision of "one like a son of man" to be a prophetic vision of Israel's Messiah—with glory, authority, and power—vindicating Israel in the victory over pagan kingdoms and sharing the throne of God, ruling an everlasting kingdom. Now, Jesus claims that he himself is this "Son of Man."

Jesus' identity is confirmed in an event that takes place about a week after Peter's confession, when Jesus takes Peter, James, and John to a high mountain. There Jesus' appearance changes as the other men watch (Mark 9:2-8; Luke 9:28-36). His face shines like the sun and his clothing becomes dazzlingly bright. For a moment the disciples see the unveiled glory and majesty of the Son of Man—the Son of God (cf. 2 Pet. 1:16-18). Moses and Elijah (Old Testament figures carrying weighty authority among the Jews) appear and stand with Jesus. God himself appears and speaks to the quivering disciples: "This is my Son, whom I love. Listen to him!" (Mark 9:7). In his glorious transfiguration and in God's own confirmation of his status, Jesus is revealed to the disciples as the One and only Son of God (Luke 9:35). For the disciples, shaken by the growing hostility of the people who hear Jesus' message, and troubled by Jesus' own ominous words about crucifixion, the way forward is clear: they must simply listen to Jesus.

Jesus Journeys to Jerusalem

Jesus' brief sojourn into Gentile territory ends, and he sets out with the disciples toward Jerusalem (Luke 9:51) for the final confrontation between the kingdom of God and the powers of darkness that lie behind Jewish opposition to the kingdom.

The Way of the Cross

As Jesus begins his last journey toward Jerusalem, he instructs the disciples further in the disturbing truth that he must suffer and be rejected, betrayed, and killed (Luke 9:22, 44; 12:49; 13:32-33; 17:25; 18:31-33). But the disciples do not yet understand (9:45).

Jerusalem will be the scene of the final battle between the kingdom of God and the powers of evil. Many in Israel expect a climactic military battle between God's army of pious Jews and the pagan Gentiles who opposed God's will. But the battle Jesus is about to face is one in which he will take the full force of cosmic evil upon himself and so exhaust its power. For Jesus, the battle will be won not by killing the enemy, but in allowing himself to be killed, to give up his life on the cross.

Discipleship in the Way of the Cross

The disciples do not understand Jesus' mission of love and suffering. Like many of their generation, they still want to see God's fiery judgment fall on those who reject his kingship (Luke 9:51-55). Even now, after all this time with Jesus, they still do not understand. Time is short; there is an urgent need for intensive training in discipleship. The disciples must truly learn what it means to follow Jesus so that after he is taken from them they will be able to continue what he has begun.

> The disciples must truly learn what it means to follow Jesus so that after he is taken from them they will be able to continue what he has begun.

This instruction on discipleship is closely tied to the theme of Jesus' last journey: he describes discipleship as a "way" to be followed, a journey to be taken. The disciples are—quite literally—on the way to Jerusalem, but at the same time they are being taught the way of discipleship. Each "way" has, as its destination, suffering and rejection. This last journey itself teaches the disciples that to follow Jesus means to walk the way of the cross.

Jesus speaks sharply to halting, half-hearted followers. The way of discipleship is costly: it demands total commitment, complete devotion, and allegiance to Jesus and the kingdom of God (9:57-62). "Whoever wants to be my disciple,"

Jesus says, "must deny themselves and take up their cross daily and follow me" (9:23; cf. 14:27). The decision to follow Jesus brings with it enormous consequences: "For whoever wants to save their life will lose it, but whoever loses their life for me will save it" (9:24).

Jesus continues by teaching his disciples that to follow him also means to participate in his mission (10:1-24). His disciples must love God with their whole being and love their neighbors as they love themselves (10:25-37). In the context of the widespread loathing within Israel for compromising Jews, Samaritans, and Gentiles, Jesus tells the story of a Jewish man beaten, robbed, and left for dead on the road from Jerusalem to Jericho. The leaders of the Jewish people—represented in Jesus' story by a priest and a Levite—do not help the man in his need. But a hated Samaritan takes pity on him and cares for him. The "righteous" Jew thus discovers that the "ungodly" Samaritan is his neighbor, the one whom God has commanded him to love.

Jesus Concludes His Kingdom Mission in Jerusalem

At last Jesus arrives in Jerusalem, where his final days are taken up with the growing hostility of the Jewish leaders and with his teaching about judgment. Upon his arrival, Jesus performs three striking actions to portray symbolically the nature of the coming kingdom—much as the Old Testament prophets dramatized God's message in remarkable symbolic actions, like Jeremiah, who smashed a pot to show that God would smash Israel (Jer. 19:1-15). Likewise, Jesus' last actions are prophetic, picturing what is to come. But because Jesus is more than a prophet, his actions mean more: he also acts as Messiah.

Jesus Enters Jerusalem on a Donkey

To celebrate the entry of a king into a city with great fanfare was a well-known phenomenon of the day. Jesus' entry into Jerusalem on a donkey proclaims louder than any words, "God is returning to Jerusalem to become King over Israel and the nations. Jesus is laying claim to David's throne." The Gospels interpret this event in the light of Zechariah 9:1-13, where Israel's king is pictured returning to Jerusalem after a military victory. As we have seen, Judah Maccabee once rode into Jerusalem to joyful shouts of praise. Yet the worldwide kingdom expected by Israel did not materialize with him. And so the Jews waited for another king to establish the universal kingdom God had promised. Other kings had come, following Judah in this practice. But none of them had brought in God's kingdom.

Against this background, Jesus' claim to Davidic kingship cannot be clearer. He enacts this same ride into Jerusalem, coming as Messiah to claim the throne of David. The crowds in Jerusalem understand this action and greet the arrival of Jesus with shouts of praise. Yet neither the crowd nor the disciples (John 12:16) understand what kind of king Jesus is. Matthew stresses in his account that Jesus comes as a gentle and humble king; his kingship is one of humble service rather than military conquest (Matt. 21:5). The animal chosen for his entry is a humble creature of burden rather than a royal war-horse. Within days, the same crowd who hails him as king will demand that he be nailed to a cross.

Jesus Enacts Judgment on the Temple

In his second messianic action in Jerusalem, Jesus visits judgment on the temple (Mark 11:12-17). Since there was always a close connection between religion and politics in the ancient Near East, the entry of a victorious king would often be followed by some kind of action in the temple. In the Gospels, the Jerusalem temple is the single most important symbol of Judaism. Above all, it stands as the center of Jewish hope for the coming kingdom. Israel believes that God will one day return to Jerusalem in fiery judgment to establish his throne and rule his worldwide kingdom (Mal. 3:1-5).

The Jerusalem crowds wait for Jesus to fulfill these expectations. But Jesus weeps because Israel has misunderstood God's coming, which indeed means judgment—not on the Gentiles, but on unfruitful Israel (Luke 19:41-44). Throughout his ministry Jesus has threatened God's judgment against God's faithless nation. When he comes in judgment against the temple, Jesus symbolically enacts all that he has been threatening.

Jesus drives out those who are selling animals for sacrifice and overturns the tables of the money-changers. Jesus temporarily shuts down operations in the temple, prefiguring its ultimate demise. And his words interpret his actions: the temple is to be a house of prayer for all nations (Mark 11:17), the place to which all people will come to acknowledge Israel's God (Isa. 56:7-8). But the temple Jesus enters now functions in a quite different way: supporting a separatist cause, encouraging violence and vengeance, it has become "a den of revolution-aries" (Mark 11:17; our translation). Judgment on this temple must take place so that a new "temple," Jesus' resurrection life in the renewed people of God (cf. John 2:21), can become the light for the nations that God intends.

When we see Jesus' cleansing of the temple in this context, it becomes clear why the Jewish leaders begin to look for a way to kill him. Not only is he challenging their treasured hopes and aspirations and announcing the destruction of their most cherished symbol, but he dares to do these things in the name of the Lord their God! This man has to go!

Jesus Dramatizes His Kingdom Mission at the Passover Meal

The week after Jesus' entry into Jerusalem is Passover week. Jesus gathers his disciples to celebrate the Passover meal together (Mark 14:12-26). This is the final and most important of the three symbolic actions Jesus performs in Jerusalem, for in this meal he dramatizes the climactic event of his kingdom mission.

On the night of Passover, Jesus directs his disciples to prepare the ritual meal, which began in Moses' time as a celebration of Israel's redemption from Egypt (Ex. 12). However, for first-century Jews it also symbolizes the coming "new exodus" by which the kingdom of God is to arrive and free the Jews from their Roman oppressors. But Jesus takes this meal and gives it new meaning. In his actions and words he says that the kingdom they long for is bursting in on them now. The climactic moment of Israel's story is to be his own death.

In the Passover tradition the head of the home interprets the events of the Exodus and their meaning for the present. Jesus thus explains in simple (but startling) words the new meaning of the bread and wine. He takes the bread, saying, "This is my body" (Mark 14:22). Jesus is about to die, and that death will mean life for his people. The cup also takes on new meaning in his words, "This is my blood of the covenant" (14:24). In his bloody death Jesus will usher in the new covenant, the forgiveness of sins, the kingdom of God for which Israel longs (cf. Jer. 31:31-34).

Jesus Is Arrested and Tried

Ever since his early ministry in Galilee attracted their attention, Jesus' enemies have been plotting his destruction (Mark 3:6). Their hostility reaches its climax with Jesus' outrageous behaviour in the temple, and they plan to arrest and kill him (14:1). One of Jesus' disciples, Judas Iscariot, appears unexpectedly and, to their great delight, offers his help: he will locate Jesus at a time when they can arrest him quietly without fear of the crowd. The Sanhedrin (the ruling council of the Jews in Jerusalem) dispatches a large group of people to carry out the arrest (14:10-11, 43).

Meanwhile, following the Passover supper, Jesus and his disciples go to a place called Gethsemane. Knowing that the final battle for the kingdom is not far off, and knowing also what horrors this will mean for him personally, Jesus prays to his Father, "Take this cup from me. Yet not what I will, but what you will" (14:36). After his prayer he rouses his sleepy disciples to face an angry crowd of Jewish leaders and soldiers led by Judas. Judas greets Jesus with a kiss, thus identifying him in the darkness. One of Jesus' followers quickly draws a sword—they still don't understand that Jesus' kingdom will come in peace, not violence (14:47). As Jesus is arrested, all but one of his disciples desert him and run for their lives (14:50-52). At a distance Peter follows the soldiers with their prisoner to see what will happen.

It is very late at night. There is a brief interrogation of the prisoner before the Jewish leaders, beginning with Annas. When Annas fails, he sends Jesus to Caiaphas (the high priest), who allows a crowd of Jewish leaders to interrogate the prisoner. False witnesses accuse Jesus of this and that, but their statements contradict one another (cf. Deut. 17:6; 19:15). In exasperation, the high priest himself finally demands, "Are you the Messiah, the Son of the Blessed One?" To which Jesus answers, "I am" (Mark 14:61-62). The court swiftly agrees that this is blasphemy deserving the death penalty (14:63-64). These middle-of-the-night interrogations are punctuated by mocking comments from onlookers and beatings from guards (14:65; Luke 22:63-65). As dawn comes and the Sanhedrin meets in formal session, they confirm the charge of blasphemy (22:66-71). During the trial, Peter is questioned about his relationship with Jesus, but three times he denies knowing him.

Since the Jews do not have the power to put anyone to death (John 18:31), Jesus is led to Pilate (the Roman-appointed procurator) for sentencing. The men of the Jewish Sanhedrin know full well that blasphemy is not a capital crime under Roman law. Instead, they charge Jesus with treason, claiming that he has been subverting Israel by opposing the payment of taxes to Caesar and by claiming to be a king (Luke 23:2).

Throughout the time he spends with Jesus, Pilate vacillates. He's unconvinced by the Jewish leaders' "charges" against Jesus, yet his own position as ruler in Palestine is already tenuous. For political reasons he cannot afford to upset the Jews. Though he can find no legal basis for passing a sentence of death against this man, he sees that the Jewish leaders will not tolerate Jesus' release. Pilate tries to duck the issue, first by sending Jesus off to Herod, then by offering the Jews an amnesty for another Jewish prisoner, Barabbas. Instigated by their leaders, the crowd cries, "Crucify him!" frustrating Pilate's attempt to reason with them. Pilate then orders that Jesus be scourged as his punishment, hoping that this will be enough for the Jews, and that he can then release the prisoner. The Roman soldiers mock and brutally scourge Jesus. After this he is returned to Pilate, who again tries to release him. The people once again chant, "Crucify him! Crucify him!" Reluctantly Pilate agrees. Sentenced to death, Jesus is led away to be nailed to a Roman cross and hang there until he dies.

> **At the cross God delivers the death blow to human sin and rebellion and accomplishes the salvation of his world.**

Jesus Dies on a Cross

In this brutal and gruesome event we see the mightiest act of God. The Bible tells of God's great deeds throughout human history to restore his creation. But when we follow the cosmic drama right up to the death and resurrection of Jesus Christ, we witness the most awesome of all God's works of redemption. At the cross God delivers the death blow to human sin and rebellion and accomplishes the salvation of his world.

Yet the crucifixion hardly seems like a victory for God, especially not when we see this event in the context of first century Roman culture.

The Romans customarily forced a condemned criminal to carry the heavy horizontal beam of his own cross to the place where he was to be crucified. But Jesus' sleepless night, the cruel mocking, and especially the brutal beatings had taken their toll. Jesus stumbles under the weight of the beam, and soldiers drag

Simon of Cyrene from the crowd, forcing him to carry it instead. The grisly parade carries on to Golgotha, "the Place of the Skull," where Jesus is offered a sedative (wine mixed with myrrh), which he refuses. At nine o'clock in the morning, Jesus is stripped naked and nailed by his wrists and feet to a cross set between two others. As the Roman soldiers drive the nails through his flesh, Jesus says, "Father, forgive them, for they do not know what they are doing" (Luke 23:34).

The soldiers write a mocking accusation on a piece of wood and fix it to the cross above his head: "This is the King of the Jews." To the Romans, calling yourself "king" was treason, an affront to Caesar's sovereignty; to the Jews it was blasphemy. But to those who can look back on this crucifixion through the lens of the resurrection that follows, the soldiers' written "accusation" is, ironically, the plain truth!

The Jewish leaders who had hounded Jesus and conspired to have him killed now heap scorn and insults on him: "He saved others . . . but he can't save himself! Let this Messiah, this king of Israel, come down now from the cross, that we may see and believe" (Mark 15:31-32). One of the criminals joins in this jeering from his own cross beside Jesus, but is rebuked by the condemned man on the other side: "We are punished justly, for we are getting what our deeds deserve. But this man has done nothing wrong." This man then turns to Jesus and says, "Jesus, remember me when you come into your kingdom" (Luke 23:40-42). Jesus acknowledges his faith; indeed, this man will inherit the kingdom of God.

At noon and for the following three hours, darkness covers the whole land. Jesus cries out in agony, "My God, my God, why have you forsaken me?" (Mark 15:34, cf. Ps. 22:1) for, at this moment, Jesus bears the sin of the world. Forsaken, Jesus does not address God as "Father," only as "my God." Then Jesus ends his epic battle with a loud cry: "It is finished!" (John 19:30), and a final prayer, "Father, into your hands I commit my spirit" (Luke 23:46). Having at last accomplished God's will, Jesus' work is complete; he can again place himself in the hands of his loving Father.

A Roman centurion stands nearby to oversee the crucifixion. When he sees the manner of Jesus' dying and hears his words, this tough professional soldier blurts out, "Surely this man was the Son of God!" (Mark 15:39). At the same moment, something strange happens back in Jerusalem, a long way from Golgotha, deep within the temple itself. There the heavy curtain that separates the holy of holies from the outer chambers, veiling the place of God's presence from the people, is torn from top to bottom, but not by human hands (15:38). The meaning is clear: the death of Jesus has opened a way into the very presence of God (cf. Heb. 4:16).

Crucifixion in the Roman Empire

"They brought Jesus to . . . Golgotha . . . and they crucified him" (Mark 15:22-24). It is difficult for us, living some two thousand years later, to comprehend just how horrifying and loathsome the idea of crucifixion was for the first-century onlooker. The unspeakable physical suffering was drawn out as long as possible—often for many hours or even days. The victim was utterly degraded, hanging naked to public view and suffering the jeers and taunts of passers by. For Roman citizens particularly, but also for subject peoples within the Roman Empire, the cross was a potent symbol of public humiliation and physical agony. It showed unforgettably just what Rome could and would do to any who dared to oppose her.

And yet the early Church had the temerity to point to this event—the crucifixion of their own leader—as the greatest of the mighty acts of God! What a ridiculous claim! How absurd to worship a crucified god!

The Romans were not alone in this opinion. The sheer horror and degradation of death by crucifixion made it virtually impossible also for Jews to accept this as an event that might reveal the hand of their God. Hadn't the Old Testament prophecies spoken of the Messiah's coming in glory and victory? But to die on a cross meant that one's life had been cursed by God (Deut. 21:23; Gal. 3:13). Moreover, the cross was the place where all those who rebelled against the Roman Empire—including many false Messiahs—ended their lives. The claim that Jesus' death was a victory must have seemed utter foolishness to almost anyone within the first-century Roman world.

Crucifixion in the New Testament

The New Testament is unique in ancient literature in interpreting the crucifixion in a positive way—as, in fact, the greatest of God's actions in history (1 Cor.

1:18 ff.). But Paul and the other New Testament writers are entirely aware that their view of this event attracts scorn; their boldness is the product of a radically different perspective, because they deliberately look back to the cross through the lens of the resurrection.

It is Jesus' return from the dead that validates his claim to be God's anointed Messiah. Looking back at the event of the cross through the lens of the resurrection, what had at first appeared to be foolishness is revealed to be the wisdom of God. What had seemed to be weakness is revealed to be the power of God, conquering human rebellion and Satanic evil. What might have been humiliation reveals the glory of God. God's self-giving love, mercy, faithfulness, grace, justice, and righteousness are shown for what they are in the event by which he accomplishes the salvation of his creation. What had seemed to the world to be Jesus' defeat is proclaimed by the early Church to be his surpassing victory over all the enemies who stand opposed to God's good creation. This apparently meaningless act of violence and cruelty in fact reveals God's fullest purpose: judgment against sin and the power and will to renew creation. In the cross, Jesus acts to accomplish God's purposes for all of history—to save the entire creation. And we can share in what God accomplished in the death of Jesus!

> This apparently meaningless act of violence and cruelty in fact reveals God's fullest purpose: judgment against sin and the power and will to renew creation. In the crossw, Jesus acts to accomplish God's purposes for all of history—to save the entire creation.

The idea that the cross is the means by which God accomplishes salvation is clear in the images the Epistles use to interpret it. The letters to young churches in the New Testament use many images to interpret the universal significance of Jesus' death. Here are three:

The first is the image of *victory*. The crucifixion is the place of the great spiritual battle between God and Satan. Jesus wins the battle and grants liberation from slavery to Satan to those for whom he fought. The second image is of *sacrifice*, and derives from the Old Testament practice in which an unblemished animal was sacrificed in place of the guilty sinner. The sinner was restored to covenant fellowship with God because that animal symbolically took away his or her sin. Now Jesus is the Lamb of God who takes away the sin of the world (John 1:29). The third image depicts Jesus as *representative man*, one who acts on behalf of an entire nation and all humankind. Jesus grapples with Satan, sin, and death and conquers them as he dies on behalf of all people. He dies for the sake of the entire cosmos, bearing God's judgment on a creation that has become corrupted and polluted by sin.

The cross represents the climactic victory of the kingdom of God. God's rule had been disrupted by human rebellion and all that came with it: demonic power, sickness, suffering, pain, and death—every kind of evil. The root of all opposition to God's rule was human rebellion, and that could be destroyed only at the cross (Rom. 8:3-4).

Jesus Rises from the Dead

After Jesus' death, Pilate gives permission to Joseph of Arimathea and Nicodemus to take the body from the cross, prepare it for burial, and lay it in a tomb. Some women who have been followers of Jesus watch to see where he is buried (Mark 15:42-47; John 19:38-42). Jesus' crucifixion naturally has left his disciples perplexed and despondent. Everything they had hoped for now seems lost. But all this soon begins to change. With the discovery of the empty tomb, the angelic announcement of the resurrection, the appearances of the risen Lord, and the testimony of those who actually see Jesus alive again, the conviction grows among his followers that Jesus is truly risen from the dead.

The women who have observed Jesus' death and burial are the first to come to the tomb to anoint his body. But instead of finding a sealed tomb, they meet two men in shining clothes! The women are naturally terrified, but one of the men calms them, then reveals that Jesus' body is no longer in the tomb: he is alive, risen from the dead.

Still trembling and bewildered—yet joyful—the women return to the city. At first they tell no one. When they do tell the other disciples, their story seems like nonsense. Nevertheless, Peter and

> For any Jew, the idea of one person being resurrected in the middle of history is inconceivable.

John go to the tomb and verify what the women have reported: the tomb is indeed empty (Luke 24:9-12; John 20:1-8). The Gospel of John tells us that the disciples still do not understand from Scripture that Jesus had to rise from the dead (20:9). For any Jew, the idea of one person being resurrected in the middle of history is inconceivable. Thus when Jesus had told them that he would rise from the dead, they had discussed among themselves what this could possibly mean (Mark 9:10).

The appearances of Jesus move his followers toward full acceptance of the truth. What we find in the Gospel record are not naive and credulous disciples who badly want to believe that Jesus is alive. Instead we find highly skeptical disciples who are only gradually convinced of the truth by Jesus' appearances to them personally. Jesus appears to Mary and the other women (John 20:11-18), to two disciples walking along the road to Emmaus (Luke 24:13-35), to the small band of disciples several times (24:36-48; John 20:19-25, 26-9; 1 Cor. 15:5), and to a larger gathering of his followers (15:6). Thus the disciples come to accept that Jesus is indeed alive, raised from the dead. But what does it all mean?

Resurrection: The Beginning of God's Renewal of Creation

What did Jesus' followers understand about resurrection? The term that we translate as "resurrection" was a vivid image in Jewish thought, implying the coming of the end of the age and the renewal of the cosmos in which God's people would participate by their own return to physical life. The idea of the resurrection of the body was therefore intricately woven together with the Jewish concept of the renewal of creation as a whole and the coming of the kingdom of God.

All the Gospels give eyewitness accounts of those who experience the living Jesus after he is bodily raised from the dead. But if this kind of thing is not supposed to happen until the end of history, what is going on? The early followers of Jesus struggle with the meaning of this new reality, seeking to interpret it "according to the Scriptures" (1 Cor. 15:4). We find their conclusions about the resurrection in their preaching in Acts, in the narratives of the four Gospels, and in the New Testament letters. The early Church joyfully proclaims the resurrection of Jesus to be the ultimate good news, an event with cosmic consequences, the beginning of God's renewal of creation.

Jesus' return from the grave is the dawn of the new day. Jesus is the first to rise again from death, but all of God's people and all of creation will share in his resurrection life. Three images in the New Testament picture the close connection between Jesus' resurrection and our own. First, Christ is the *firstborn* from the dead (Col. 1:18; Rev. 1:5). His siblings (believers like you and me) will follow their elder brother in his new life. Second, Christ is described as the *firstfruits* (1 Cor. 15:20, 23), the first part of the agricultural harvest to be brought in, as a kind of guarantee that the whole harvest is to follow. Third, Jesus is pictured as the *pioneer* of our salvation (Heb. 2:10), the one who goes ahead into new territory to lead the way and mark the trail. Jesus has led the way for us into the age to come and marked our path into the kingdom of God. We come into that resurrection life as we follow him, first in foretaste (on this side of the completed kingdom) and at last entering it fully (on the new earth).

Jesus Commissions His Disciples

After the resurrection, Jesus gathers his disciples and charges them to carry on the task that he has begun. Each of the Gospels looks at this last commission in a different way, according to its intended audience. Matthew reports these words from the risen Christ: "All authority in heaven and on earth has been given to me" (28:18). Matthew underscores the cosmic scope of Jesus' authority with a fourfold repetition of the word "all." Jesus is given *all* authority. His followers are to make disciples of *all* nations. They are to teach the disciples to obey *all* Jesus has commanded. And Jesus will be working among them *all* the days that remain for the earth (28:18-20). Through the unpretentious but amazingly effective mission of the Church in making disciples, the exalted Christ, the Lord with all authority, will "subdue" his enemies—in love. The former "enemy" is then baptized into the community of disciples and there taught the way of Jesus.

In the Gospel of John, Jesus is portrayed as the one sent by the Father into the world to bring life. On the evening of resurrection Sunday, Jesus appears among his disciples and tells them to continue what he has been doing: "As the Father has sent me, I am sending you" (John 20:21). In the same way that Jesus himself carried out his mission, the newly gathered community is to carry out its mission, continuing to bring his life into a needy world.

In the Gospel of Luke, Jesus commissions the disciples to be "witnesses," a word from the justice system identifying someone called to testify to what he or she has experienced. This new community is expected to testify, first to the death and resurrection of Jesus Christ, and then to his offer of repentance and forgiveness for all people. Again, Luke emphasizes that this witness cannot begin until the Father has sent the promised Spirit and clothed Jesus' followers with the power they will need to carry out the task (Luke 24:46-49; cf. Acts 1:8).

The Climax of the Biblical Story

Jesus' entry into human history—his earthly life, his death, and his resurrection from the dead—marks the climax of the biblical story. Jesus reveals the coming kingdom in his public ministry. At the cross he conquers evil itself. The new day of resurrection for all creation dawns when Jesus rises from the dead. Does this mean the kingdom of God is about to come immediately in its fullness? His followers certainly thought so, at least initially (Acts 1:6). But if the coming of the kingdom was not to be immediate—what then? How should followers of Jesus live in the meantime? What should they do? The commission that ends the Gospels give us a clue.

> **The new day of resurrection for all creation dawns when Jesus rises from the dead.**

While Matthew, Mark, and John end their stories of Jesus with the resurrection, Luke continues his narrative in the book of Acts. We will turn to this book next for the answers to the disciples' early questions about the timing of his kingdom's coming and their own place—and ours—in his continuing mission.

Reflections for Today

Just as the cross and resurrection stand at the climax of the true story of the whole world, they are the compass bearings by which we live today. Suffering love conquers sin and death. Through an ignominious cross God reclaims his reign over the cosmos. We are Easter people, followers of the risen Lord. That changes everything.

In the early 1920s a Communist leader, Nikolai Bukharin, was sent from Moscow to Kiev to address an anti-God rally. For an hour he abused and ridiculed the Christian faith. Then questions were invited. An Orthodox Church priest rose and asked to speak. He turned, faced the people, and gave the Easter greeting "He is risen!" Instantly the assembly rose to its feet and the reply came back loud and clear: "He is risen indeed!"

For a world so twisted by evil and enslaved by sin, what other message offers true hope? He is risen! In the resurrection of Jesus Christ, a new world is dawning. The resurrection stands at the center of the Christian faith.

Now the risen Lord calls us to follow him today. "As the Father has sent me, I am sending you." These words of Jesus help to focus our questions and find our place in the story. What did the Father send Jesus to do? How did he do it? As we consider how the gospel story works itself out in our own lives, our focus should be upon Jesus himself, who made known the coming kingdom of God in his own life, words, and deeds. We are called to follow Jesus; to do in our time and culture what he did in his. That takes imagination and creativity. We don't thoughtlessly or naively imitate Jesus; rather, we struggle to discern how we can creatively, imaginatively, and faithfully translate what Jesus did into our cultural setting.

We must ask ourselves, "What are the different aspects of Jesus' kingdom mission?" and "How can we creatively follow Jesus today?" If we truly follow Jesus, we hold up the light of God's kingdom in a world where people around us stumble in the darkness.

Lesslie Newbigin gives an illustration of this from his own experience in India. Walking eastward to another village, setting out before the sunrise (while it is still cool enough to walk a distance), Newbigin met other travellers on the road walking in the opposite direction. And though the night was not yet quite over, the faces of Newbigin and others travelling with him actually shone in the darkness. They were walking toward the east, and the first light of dawn was reflected in them. As long as the other travellers continued on their own way toward the west, they could not see the source of that light for themselves. They were facing the wrong way. But they knew the light was coming, because they saw it in the eastward-bound travellers' faces.

Many in our own world are travelling in the wrong direction. But if the Church keeps its own eyes fixed on Jesus and his kingdom, seeking to incarnate his life in the contemporary world, we will reflect his light in our lives. And perhaps those whom we meet along the way will turn to see the light for themselves.

Finding Our Place in the Story

1. Jesus taught that God's loving purpose was to restore the whole of creation under his gracious authority: he called it the "kingdom of God." Since this term is not as easily understood today, what language can we use to communicate this great truth?

2. Jesus embodied the kingdom in his whole way of living. Discuss how Jesus' life is a pattern for us in the following:

   • intimate relationship with the Father
   • dependence on the Holy Spirit
   • prayer
   • joy
   • pursuit of justice

3. What other aspects of Jesus' life do you see as important for us to learn from and to imitate?

4. We have seen how Jesus had special concern for the poor, the marginalized, the outcast. How can we follow Jesus in this path? Who are the poor and marginalized today?

5. Jesus suffered as he stood up against the idolatrous powers that shaped Jewish and Roman culture. What idolatrous powers shape modern secular culture? How might we be called to suffer today for the sake of following Jesus?

6. How did reading about the horror of the cross affect you? What does it mean for us to "take up our cross and follow" Jesus?

7. What did Jesus accomplish on the cross? Why is it such an important part of the drama of Scripture? How is it important in your own story?

8. "I believe that on the third day Jesus rose from the dead." What is the significance of this confession? Is it more than simply believing a historical fact?

9. In the last pages of the Gospels, Jesus gives his Church its "marching orders" (Matt. 28:18-20; John 20:21; Luke 24:46-49; Acts 1:8). How should this "commission" shape the life of the Church today?

Act 5

Spreading the News of the King— The Mission of the Church

Scene 1: From Jerusalem to Rome

n his death Jesus conquered sin, and in his resurrection he inaugurated a new era of salvation. The kingdom banquet is ready to be enjoyed, but it does not begin just yet. More peoples must first be gathered to the banquet table. This in-between time—after Jesus' first coming and before he comes again—is a time for the great gathering of the nations, the mission of the exalted Christ, the Spirit, and the Church. And it's here that the story continues right into our lives today.

Of the four Gospels' writers, only Luke carries the story past Jesus' death and resurrection. The book of Acts forms the second volume of Luke's Gospel, telling the story of the coming of God's kingdom during the three decades following Jesus' resurrection.

Christ, ascended and reigning at God's right hand, now pours out his salvation on the world. Luke's opening words in the book of Acts suggest this mission: "In my former book, Theophilus, I wrote about all that Jesus *began* to do and teach until the day he was taken up to heaven" (Acts 1:1-2, italics ours). Luke clearly implies that this second volume of his story will tell of all that Jesus *continues* to do and teach, even after he has returned to the Father. Jesus will now work primarily through his Spirit, poured out on the church at Pentecost. While he was alive visibly on earth, Jesus mostly confined his work to Israel; the exalted Christ now extends his ministry "to the ends of the earth" (1:8). So this second volume of the gospel tells the story of the continued mission of the exalted Christ, by the work of his Spirit, to give salvation to the Church—and through the Church to the whole world. We who stand in historical continuity with that early Church are also swept up in this mission. Their story is also our story.

Christ Is Exalted to the Right Hand of God

As the book of Acts begins, the risen Christ appears to his disciples over a period of forty days, during which time there is much talk of the kingdom of God and the coming of the Spirit (Acts 1:3-5). The disciples ask Jesus the obvious question: "Lord, are you at this time going to restore the kingdom to Israel?" (1:6). His answer is significant: "It is not for you to know the times or dates the Father has set by his own authority. But you will receive power when the Holy Spirit comes on you; and you will be my witnesses in Jerusalem, and in all Judea and Samaria, and to the ends of the earth" (1:7-8). It is not for the disciples to know when the end will come (cf. Mark 13:32), but until Jesus returns the Spirit will bring the life of the kingdom through the witness of Jesus' followers to all nations.

> **This is coronation day! The Messiah now shares the throne of God over all creation and all peoples.**

Then Jesus is taken up into heaven (Acts 1:9), or "exalted to the right hand of God," as Peter says later (2:33; 5:31). This is coronation day! The Messiah now shares the throne of God over all creation and all peoples.

The name given to Jesus as he ascends to rule from God's right hand is significant. An early Christian confession states:

> God exalted [Jesus] to the highest place
> and gave him the name that is above every name,
> that at the name of Jesus every knee should bow,
> in heaven and on earth and under the earth,
> and every tongue acknowledge that Jesus Christ is Lord,
> to the glory of God the Father (Phil. 2:9-11).

This "name" becomes the central confession of the early Church: Jesus is Lord, a title that speaks of supreme authority—*kyrios* in Greek (Acts 2:36; Rom. 10:9; 1 Cor. 12:3). In the Roman Empire Caesar was supreme Lord. Roman military commanders and others were required to testify, "Caesar is Lord." But the early Church could not say this. Jesus—not Caesar—is Lord over all the earth! The early Church's refusal to say otherwise set them on a collision course with Roman authority and led to much conflict and suffering.

When Peter (in Acts 2:32-36) says that Jesus has been raised to the right hand of God, he quotes Psalm 110:1: "The Lord said to my Lord: 'Sit at my right hand until I make your enemies a footstool for your feet.'" This verse defines the mission of the exalted Christ: to subdue all his enemies. In the remainder of the psalm it seems that God's kingdom will come by violent military power over Israel's political enemies. Yet Jesus uses his authority in a very different way.

In his earlier teaching, Jesus redefined both the meaning of the word "enemies" and what it would mean to "defeat" them. The real enemies of God's kingdom were not the Romans but the spiritual powers of evil that stand behind all opposition to God's rule. The final defeat of evil came not by military force but by the sacrificial love of the cross. Jesus "subdues" his human enemies as they begin to participate in the salvation he has accomplished.

The Exalted Christ Pours out His Spirit

After Jesus ascends to the Father, his work continues with the outpouring of his Spirit. The Old Testament promised that in the last days the Spirit would be "poured out"—on the Servant Messiah (Isa. 42:1), on Israel (Ezek. 37:14), and at last on all people (Joel 2:28-32). After the resurrection, Jesus says that this promised Holy Spirit will be poured out on his followers, and then he tells them to wait in Jerusalem until this happens (Luke 24:49; Acts 1:4-5).

This mighty act of God occurs about ten days after Jesus' ascension, on the Jewish Feast of Pentecost. In Jesus' day the Feast of Pentecost celebrated the covenant renewal of Israel and the inclusion of the nations within the covenant made between God and Israel. Now, at this first Pentecost after Christ's resurrection, the Spirit comes to fulfil that expectation and hope.

As Jesus' disciples gather on the day of Pentecost, the sound of a violent wind suddenly fills the house (Acts 2:1-4). What looks like tongues of fire rest on their heads, and all are filled with the Holy Spirit. Wind represents the power of God to bring new life (Ezek. 37:9, 14)—the same Hebrew and Greek words can mean "spirit," "breath," or "wind," depending on the context. Fire often represents the presence of God, as it did to Moses at the burning bush, or to Israel at Mount

Sinai (Ex. 3:2; 13:21-22; 19:18). Here at Pentecost the Spirit comes in wind and fire as the powerful presence of God bringing the life of the kingdom.

During the Feast of Pentecost, people from all over the Roman Empire fill Jerusalem. A third sign of the Spirit's presence—after wind and fire—comes when the disciples begin to speak in different languages, making the good news available to all these strangers in their own tongues. God's message in these signs is clear: the gospel is no longer confined to the Jewish nation and the Hebrew language.

This remarkable event bewilders those who witness it. What can be happening? Peter stands up and delivers a sermon that answers this question (Acts 2:14-36): God is fulfilling Joel's prophecy that the Spirit will be poured out in the last days (2:16-21). These "last days" have arrived, ushered in by the life, death, resurrection, and exaltation of Jesus of Nazareth. He is Lord and Messiah. Having received the promised Holy Spirit from his Father, Christ has now poured out the same Spirit on his disciples.

The exalted Christ will now work by his Spirit, who thus becomes the primary actor in the book of Acts, to bring good news to the ends of the earth. The Spirit's first work is to form a community to share in the salvation of the kingdom and to be a channel of that salvation to others (2:37-47).

The Spirit Forms a Community

When Peter concludes his sermon explaining how God is at work among them, the people respond by asking, "What shall we do?" Peter replies, "Repent and be baptized, every one of you, in the name of Jesus Christ for the forgiveness of your sins. And you will receive the gift of the Holy Spirit" (Acts 2:38). God requires those who respond to him to repent—to turn from idolatry and re-orient their lives to Christ's coming kingdom—and be baptized into this community that now has received the gift of the kingdom: the Holy Spirit. Responding to Peter's sermon, about three thousand people "were added to their number that day" (2:41). Luke goes on to describe the life of this early church community (2:42-47), a blueprint for what the Church ought to be in every age.

This young Church has three defining qualities. First, it centers its life on what will bring the life of the Spirit to itself: the apostles' teaching, fellowship, the breaking of bread, and prayer. By these means, the young Church experiences more and more the life of the kingdom (2:42). Second, the life of Christ is manifested both in the lives of individual members of the young Church and in the life of the community as a whole. The Church becomes known by convincing signs of God's saving power within it (2:43), by justice and mercy in its communal relations (2:44-45), by joyful conviviality (2:46), and by worship (2:47). Third, as the liberating life of the kingdom becomes more and more evident in the Church, we hear that the exalted Lord "[adds] to their number daily those who are being saved" (2:47). Note that Luke attributes this growth to the Lord's power and life in the church. This too fulfills Old Testament prophecies about God's kingdom. The prophets picture the drawing power of a renewed Israel (Isa. 60:2-3; Zech. 8:20-23). The life and power of the Spirit of Christ in the believing community radiates the light of the kingdom and draws people in from the darkness.

> The life and power of the Spirit of Christ in the believing community radiates the light of the kingdom and draws people in from the darkness.

The Church Witnesses in Jerusalem

The story of the Church's witness continues in Jerusalem (Acts 3:1-6:7), reaches outward to Judea and Samaria (6:8-11:18), and eventually moves from the fringes and provinces of the Roman Empire to Rome itself (11:19-28:31), as Jesus himself had promised (1:8). Acts 3:1-6:7 tells more about the first stage of this witness of the Spirit through the apostolic community—the beginnings, in Jerusalem.

Note the three agents of this witness: it is the work, first, of the exalted Christ; second, of the Spirit; and third, of the Church. The book of Acts describes how these three agents all act through the word of God. In each major section of Acts we read the clause, "So the word of God spread," or something similar (6:7; 12:24; 19:20). The gospel message spreads from Jerusalem to Rome, gathering an increasing number of followers as it is embodied in their community, enacted in their lives, and explained in their words.

After God pours out the Spirit (2:1-13), the first believing community is formed in Jerusalem in response to Peter's proclamation of the good news (2:14-47). This band of believers follows Jesus by witnessing to the kingdom, just as he did. In Luke's account this witness by the believers' deeds as well as their words begins when Peter and John visit the temple and heal a man crippled from birth (3:1-10). This immediately draws a crowd, and Peter takes the opportunity to proclaim the good news once more (3:11-26).

The words and actions of these two disciples immediately bring a hostile reaction and suffering, just as Jesus' own words and actions had done. The Jewish leaders arrest Peter and John, put them in jail, and then bring them before the Sanhedrin to account for their "disruptive" preaching. Eventually they're released with a warning.

After their release, Peter and John return to the church community to report what has taken place, and the church immediately turns to prayer. They ask the Sovereign Lord to grant them continued boldness and power in their witness in the face of hostility (4:23-31). The result is dramatic: "After they prayed, the place where they were meeting was shaken. And they were all filled with the Holy Spirit and spoke the word of God boldly" (4:31).

As more and more people believe and are added to the number of Christ's followers (5:14), the success of this movement fills the Jewish leaders with jealousy. Their reprisals escalate from verbal abuse to floggings. But the apostles receive this brutal treatment with joy, because they have been counted worthy to suffer for the name of Jesus (5:41). Their witness continues: "Day after day, in the temple courts and from house to house, they never stopped teaching and proclaiming the good news that Jesus is the Messiah" (5:42). Mere human opposition cannot stop the spread of the gospel because the growth of the Church and the coming of the kingdom are the work of God. Neither the Sanhedrin nor Herod nor any other political authority can silence the powerful witness of the gospel (3; 5; 12).

Much of Acts is taken up with the witness of the apostles. Yet it is the life of the community as it embodies the powerful working of the Spirit that authenticates the truth of the good news. That vibrant and sharing life attracts more and more people from outside the community to join with those who already possess this new life. The apostolic witness depends on a community that verifies the truth of the gospel with its winsome lifestyle (4:32-35).

The disciples' witness to the good news in Jerusalem and the gathering of a believing community fulfills Old Testament prophecies about gathering scattered Israel. But the same prophecies had also promised that God's salvation would extend to all nations. At this point in its story the early Church remains largely a Jewish community (though some Gentiles are beginning to join). In the next important development, the gospel moves increasingly to those outside the Jewish context, beginning with God-fearing Gentiles who already worship in the synagogue.

The Church Witnesses in Samaria and Judea

The good news of the kingdom cannot remain locked up in Jerusalem. It must reach "to the ends of the earth." As the gospel spreads from Jerusalem and into the provinces of Judea and Samaria (Acts 6:8-12:24), the responsibility for witness moves beyond the apostles to include others in the community. Luke especially highlights the ministry of Stephen and Philip, who are among the seven leaders appointed in the Jerusalem church (6:1-6). Stephen's witness brings further opposition, and eventually he becomes the first one to die for the gospel.

Great persecution then breaks out against the church in Jerusalem. Disciples leave for the surrounding areas of Judea and Samaria. But "those who had been scattered preached the word wherever they went" (8:4). Though the Church certainly had not planned this "missionary expansion," the Spirit used the scattering to spread the good news. No longer do only the official spokesmen of the church make the gospel known (8:4; 1 Thess. 1:8). Now ordinary believers, the informal "missionaries" of the early Church, begin to spontaneously tell the good news to their friends and neighbors.

> Now ordinary believers, the informal "missionaries" of the early Church, begin to spontaneously tell the good news to their friends and neighbors.

Undoubtedly the single most important event in this period of persecution is the conversion and call of God on the life of Saul, a man from Tarsus (Acts 9:1-30). Saul, who was present when Stephen was stoned to death, now leads the Sanhedrin's campaign of persecution against the young Church. He sets out to capture disciples of Jesus and return them to Jerusalem for trial. However, on the road to Damascus a blinding light strikes Saul, and he hears a voice saying,

"Saul, Saul, why do you persecute me?" After Saul asks, "Who are you, Lord?" he hears, "I am Jesus, whom you are persecuting" (9:4-5). From this moment, Saul becomes a follower of Jesus Christ. He will play an important role in the spread of the gospel to Gentiles as the Lord's "chosen instrument to carry [Jesus'] name to the Gentiles and their kings and to the people of Israel" (9:15).

The gospel spreads beyond Jerusalem mostly through Jewish synagogues throughout Palestine and beyond. So the very early Church maintains its close association with Jewish religion and culture. But that is about to change, and the change begins with Peter.

Following a vision in which the Lord dramatically confirms that the gospel must go to the Gentiles (10:9-23), Peter is summoned to the house of Cornelius, a Gentile. There Peter tells the good news of Jesus to a Gentile household. While he is speaking, the Spirit falls upon all those listening, and Peter and the other Jewish Christians are astonished to see for themselves that God pours out the Spirit even on Gentiles. Cornelius and his household then are baptized in the name of Jesus (10:44-48). When Peter returns to Jerusalem, the church community there criticizes him for eating with Gentiles. Peter explains the visions he and Cornelius have received, and the fact that the Spirit himself has ratified the faith of these Gentiles. After that, the Jewish believers in the Jerusalem church have no further objections (11:1-17). They praise God that he has granted even to Gentiles "repentance that leads to life" (11:18).

The Church Witnesses to the Ends of the Earth

Though the gospel has begun to move outside of Jerusalem, it was mostly among the Jews scattered throughout the Roman Empire or to God-fearing Gentiles. But something new begins to take place in Antioch, where believers—both Jews and Gentiles—have come together to form a church community (Acts 11:19-21). This church is destined to become the base for a large-scale missionary project that will send Paul to many parts of the Roman Empire. While the church at Antioch is worshiping and fasting, the Holy Spirit speaks to them: "Set apart for me Barnabas and Saul for the work to which I have called them" (13:2). After more fasting and prayer, the leaders of the church place their hands on Saul and Barnabas as a sign of their solidarity with what these two will do, and then send them off to preach the gospel in other cities of the Roman Empire.

Here for the first time we see a planned effort to take the gospel to places where it has not yet been heard. The Antioch church still carries out its own mission locally in the place where it has been set. But now it also envisions a mission to "the ends of the earth" in obedience to God's calling. The first major move outward from Jerusalem had been an unplanned expansion of the gospel into Judea, Samaria, and certain Gentile areas (6:8-12:25). Now we see organized expansion from the church at Antioch into Asia Minor and Europe under Paul's leadership (12:25-19:20).

Paul, the great Christian missionary figure, was introduced to us as Saul the Pharisee, the ruthless persecutor of the Church in its early days. After Saul's vision of the risen Christ, he experienced a dramatic conversion and answered God's call to be "a light for the Gentiles" and to "bring salvation to the ends of the earth" (13:47). This man becomes the central human witness of the gospel story in Acts from chapter 13 to the end, and thirteen letters in the New Testament have his name on them.

Paul's missionary work includes planting new churches and building them up to radiate the light of the gospel. His goal is to establish witnessing kingdom communities in every part of the Roman Empire (Rom. 15:17-23). He also takes time to establish these communities on a firm foundation. Paul teaches the gospel through the Old Testament Scriptures, establishes leadership to oversee the community's growth, and institutes the Lord's Supper. Often in his travels he returns to "strengthen" the churches he has founded or built up (Acts 15:41). He also writes letters (or epistles) to these young churches for the same purpose, letters that are now part of our New Testament.

Paul makes three journeys to plant and build up churches in Asia Minor, Greece, and Macedonia, always taking various traveling companions with him. In his first journey, Paul travels from Antioch to Cyprus and on into cities in Asia Minor (modern Turkey) before returning to Antioch to make his report to the sending church (14:24-28).

On his first missionary trip, Paul's habit was to begin by preaching first in the synagogues along the way, since, as a learned Jew, he was deeply familiar with the Old Testament prophecies that God's renewal is to start with Israel (Rom. 1:16).

Many Jews whom he encounters there oppose his preaching, but many others come to believe the gospel message. Then, as Jewish resistance intensifies, Paul moves outward from the synagogue community to bring the same message directly to the Gentiles, who are often

The churches Paul plants and nurtures in his first journey come to be made up mostly of Gentile believers.

receptive. So the churches Paul plants and nurtures in his first journey come to be made up mostly of Gentile believers.

It may be difficult for us today to understand how hard it was for the Jews of the first century to give up traditions that had for so long safeguarded their religious identity as distinct from the pagan Gentiles. Paul now calls them to accept Gentile believers as equal partners in this renewed "Israel" of God's kingdom.

Not surprisingly, struggles among Jewish Christians themselves over the inclusion of Gentiles mark this early period of the Church's story. A group of Jewish Christians from Jerusalem even began to travel from place to place in Galatia, visiting churches planted there by Paul and attempting to convince Gentile Christians that they should live as if they were Jews. But Paul fires off an angry and impassioned letter to the Galatian churches, urging them rather to remain constant in their faith: salvation is in Christ alone, not in the works of the law. This crucial struggle builds until a council held in Jerusalem concludes that Gentiles should be admitted to the Church as equal members (Acts 15). Though this decision brings peace for a time within the churches, the controversy lingers for some time.

Paul's second journey (15:36-18:22) is notable for two reasons. First, he changes his strategy somewhat. He chooses to spend more time in each region's important cities, soundly establishing churches there. Second, on this journey he visits churches in most of the places that will eventually receive one of his pastoral letters: Philippi, Thessalonica, Corinth, and Ephesus.

On Paul's third journey his primary goal is to establish a church in the strategically important city of Ephesus (which he visited briefly at the end of his second journey). Paul successfully plants a church there, but also challenges the flourishing occult practices and pagan worship in that important city. He stays on at Ephesus for over two years (19:1-41), during which time "the word of the

Lord [spreads] widely and [grows] in power" (19:20). While in Ephesus, Paul writes at least four letters to the church at Corinth (two of which have been preserved in our Bible), addressing a number of questions about what it means to embody the gospel in the pagan setting of Corinth.

Upon leaving Ephesus, Paul travels back toward Jerusalem, stopping for three months in Greece, from where he writes to the Christians at Rome. This letter to the Romans has probably had more influence in Church history than any other. Because Paul has never visited Rome, the tone in this letter is more formal as he deepens the Roman Christians' understanding of the gospel and of the relationship between Jews and Gentiles.

Paul finishes his last journey by visiting the church in Jerusalem, where he reports on his missionary endeavours (21:17-26). In Jerusalem, Paul is arrested by the Romans at the instigation of the Jewish authorities (21:27-36). The remainder of the book of Acts shows Paul in his various judicial hearings and trials, as he moves from Jerusalem to Caesarea and then on to Rome. Even these trials afford Paul opportunities to proclaim the good news to many, including various rulers (cf. 9:15). During his time in Rome, he writes letters to the churches in Philippi, Ephesus, and Colossae, and also to Philemon, the owner of a runaway slave whom Paul had led to Christ. Luke ends his story of the work of Jesus in the young Church by telling us that Paul spends two years in Rome under house arrest, boldly preaching about the kingdom of God and the Lord Jesus Christ. Though the end of Paul's life is not recorded in the Bible, historians believe he was executed in Rome by order of the violently anti-Christian emperor Nero.

Paul Unfolds the Gospel in His Letters

Paul plays a highly significant role in the biblical story. He is the central human figure in the latter part of Acts, bringing the gospel from its original Jewish setting out into the Gentile world. Paul is above all a "missionary," one who is sent to take the good news to places where it has not yet been heard. Paul also has a missionary pastor's heart. He longs to see each of the churches he has planted flourish and become a vibrant, witnessing community that faithfully points to the coming kingdom of God in life, word, and deed. If we are to understand Paul's teaching in his letters, we must see him first as a missionary pastor.

Paul's letters unfold the significance of the good news of Jesus Christ for individual churches in particular historical situations. They build on, flow from, and explain the good news of what God has done for the world in the life, death, and resurrection of Jesus Christ. Paul unfolds in detail the meaning of the good news and its implications for the Church's new life in Christ. Each of Paul's letters addresses a different church with its own problems and questions. In the scope of this book we can only briefly describe the basic tenets of Paul's teaching.

The Kingdom of God Has Dawned in Christ

As a brilliant young Pharisee, Saul of Tarsus had been taught to think of human history as divided between the present age and the age to come. In Jewish thinking, the present age was dominated by sin, evil, and death, but in the age to come God would return to Israel and usher in his kingdom. When a group of people in Jerusalem began to make the claim that in the crucified Jesus this kingdom had already come, Saul was incensed. But everything changed when the risen Jesus personally confronted him. If Jesus was the Jewish Messiah who arose from the dead, that meant the age to come had dawned; the kingdom of God was here already. And thus the newborn Christian and former Pharisee found himself rethinking all he thought he knew.

This is Paul's starting point: the kingdom of God, the age to come, has arrived in the death and resurrection of Jesus Christ. Two great figures stand at the entrances to two ages and two worlds: Adam stands at the gate of the old world, Jesus at the gate of the new. Adam's first sin inaugurated the old age and brought sin, death, and condemnation; in Jesus, a new day of righteousness, life, and justification has come (Rom. 5:12-21). If we are "in Adam," we are part of the old age and under its sway. But if we are "in Christ," we are part of the age to come and can already experience God's life-giving power here and now.

> This is Paul's starting point: the kingdom of God, the age to come, has arrived in the death and resurrection of Jesus Christ.

The resurrection of Jesus is the explosive event that prompts the great change in Paul's thinking about the kingdom. On the road to Damascus the risen Jesus had met Saul face-to-face. To Saul, thinking as a carefully trained Jew of the first century, resurrection meant rising bodily into the life of the age to come. But since Jesus was clearly alive again, that must mean that the kingdom had come already. The age "to come" had arrived. Thus Paul describes the risen Jesus as the firstborn among many brothers and sisters (8:29), the firstfruits of those who have died (1 Cor. 15:20).

For Paul, this new view of the resurrection demands a similarly new view of the crucifixion. From the Old Testament he had learned, "cursed is everyone who is hung on a pole" (Gal. 3:13; cf. Deut. 21:23). But since this Jesus is the Messiah, and since God has raised him from the dead, Paul recognizes that the cross itself must be reexamined through the lens of the resurrection. Since the resurrection means the beginning of the new age and the entrance to the new world, Christ's crucifixion must mean the end of the old age and the old world (Rom. 6:1-11). For the sake of the world, Christ had taken upon himself God's curse, the guilt and power of sin that had ruled the old age (Gal. 3:13-14). The cross marks God's victory over the powers of sin and evil that had been ruling the world in the present age (Col. 2:15).

But if the old has passed away and the new has come, why do evil and death remain in the world? Paul's letters are charged with the same tension between the "already" but "not yet" aspects of the kingdom of God that we have seen in Jesus' own teachings, but with some differences in emphasis. For Paul, the kingdom is here already in that Jesus' death brings an end to the old and his resurrection inaugurates the new. The Spirit is described as a deposit (or down payment) on the coming kingdom (2 Cor. 1:22; 5:5; Eph. 1:14). A deposit is not merely an IOU or promise for the future; it is a real payment given now as a guarantee that in the future the rest will be paid. The Spirit is also pictured as firstfruits, the first part of the harvest, ready to be enjoyed now and tangible evidence that the remainder of the harvest will also come (Rom. 8:23).

The kingdom has not yet arrived for us in its fullness. We remain in a world that has not yet been fully delivered from the influence of the powers of evil (2 Cor. 4:4). The dark powers of sin and rebellion against God still surround us (Eph. 2:2-3), even while we anticipate the full revelation of God's kingdom when those things shall be no more. We live in the "in between" time in which the two ages overlap. Paul goes on to explain that these two ages are allowed to coexist within God's plan so that the Church's work of mission—the gathering of the nations to the God of Israel—can be accomplished before the final revelation of the kingdom.

Nurturing the Growth of Our New Life in Christ

As we have seen, Paul's first concern as a missionary is to bring the gospel where it has not yet been heard. For Paul, the gospel is the very power of God to bring salvation, to bring men and women into the kingdom of the age to come. So Paul is always eager, even compelled, to tell the gospel story (Rom. 1:14-15; 1 Cor. 9:16). As his hearers respond in faith and are baptized to signify their "death" to the old way of life and their "resurrection" to new life in Christ among his people, new-born churches are established wherever Paul travels through the Roman Empire.

But these infant churches cannot simply be left to fend for themselves. They are bearing witness to the reality of God's kingdom as they live out their lives in the present age, facing the evil still at work in the world before the kingdom comes in its fullness. So Paul's second concern as a missionary is to bring these communities of believers to maturity in their faith and witness. Paul especially uses two images to capture this process of coming to maturity. First, he pictures the Church as the new temple of God, where God now lives by the Holy Spirit (1 Cor. 3:16; Eph. 2:21-22). Its foundation is the gospel itself and it comes to maturity as it builds on that foundation (Eph. 4:12). Second, Paul likens the Church's coming to maturity to the organic growth of a human body from infancy to adulthood (4:15) or of a field crop (1 Cor. 3:5-9) "rooted" in Jesus Christ (Eph. 3:17; Col. 2:7) and being cared for so that it might come to fruitful maturity.

The Church's life begins by receiving the life of the Spirit through the gospel: it is founded on Christ and rooted in him. But the community continues to grow by faith in the gospel (Gal. 3:2-3; Col. 2:6-7) as believers are nurtured by the Spirit toward maturity, adulthood, and fruitfulness. Since Christ is the second Adam, the new human being, believers grow up into him and become like him (Eph. 4:11-16). Paul discusses at length the various gifts and ministries given to the Church by the Spirit to bring it to fullness.

New Life and New Obedience

Moving toward fullness in Christ is an ongoing task. Paul therefore repeatedly urges the newly established churches to live a life worthy of the gospel, but it is important to notice the pattern of his moral exhortation. First he tells these young Christians what God has done to give them new life, their new identity as the people of God through faith and baptism. Then he tells them what they must do to live according to that new identity. Since God has given them new life in the kingdom of God, they are to live as obedient citizens of that kingdom. In other words, they are to become what they already are.

The churches' new life is based on what God has done in the death and resurrection of Jesus Christ. In Christ's death, God has defeated the powers that rule this present age: sin, evil, and death. In Christ's resurrection the "age to come" has begun with its promise of life, love, and peace (Rom. 6:1-11). The churches' new life is also empowered by the Spirit, which lives within the community of believers and constantly brings new life to it (Rom. 8; Gal. 5).

At the heart of this new life is a new relationship to God, which Paul describes in terms of righteousness, reconciliation, and adoption. According to the law— God's perfect standard of right—all of us who trace our ancestry to Adam have come short of perfection and been found guilty. But in Christ that guilty verdict has been overturned, and we are now declared righteous: we stand again in a right relationship to God. Our alienation from God has been removed and we are reconciled to him. We are adopted into God's family. We may now call God "*Abba*, Father," as Jesus did (Rom. 8:14-15).

> This is the Church: a people who live in a new world with a new identity and a new relationship to God.

This is the Church: a people who live in a new world with a new identity and a new relationship to God. Thus Paul commands the Church to live more and more the new life of God's kingdom, to "take off" the old self (as if it were soiled clothing) and put on the new (Eph. 4:22-24; Col. 3:9-10). In other words, believers are to bid farewell to the way of life that was shaped by their experience of this present age and embrace a new way of life as part of the age to come.

This call to obedience embraces the restoration of the whole of human life. Christ rules over all creation and redeems all creation (1:15-20). Thus all human life, including even the mundane activities like eating and drinking, should be lived to the glory of God (1 Cor. 10:31). Since the whole of our bodily life is to be devoted to God (Rom. 6:13; 12:1-2), whatever we do in word or deed should be done in the name of the Lord Jesus, giving thanks to God the Father (Col. 3:17). Paul also roots this comprehensive obedience in the goodness of the creation, which is being redeemed with us (1 Cor. 10:26; 1 Tim. 4:1-5). But Paul is also aware that the whole of human life, though it was created by God and has been redeemed by Christ, still suffers from the pollution of sin. So he warns believers that, though they have liberty to enjoy God's good creation, they must be careful not to be contaminated by the sin that infects it (1 Cor. 6:12).

The standard for behavior for the Church's new life of obedience in Christ remains the law of God given in the Old Testament (Rom. 8:3-4). But Paul also recognizes, as Jesus taught, that love stands at the heart of the law (Rom. 13:8, 10; Gal. 5:14). This love, coming as the "fruit" of the new life of the Spirit, takes many forms; in Paul's letters, love is often bound together with joy and peace to form a triad (as in Rom. 5:1-8). Love also comes through in other characteristic qualities of the kingdom: humility, patience, kindness, goodness, faithfulness, gentleness, self-control, righteousness, and gratitude (see Gal. 5:22-23).

For the Sake of the World

The Church exhibits this new life and obedience for the sake of the world. When the Church's new life of the Spirit becomes evident to unbelievers, they too will be convinced of the truth of this "good news" and so be drawn to Christ. As Paul struggles to nurture a community that faithfully embodies the new life of the kingdom, he always has his eye on those outside the Church. In describing the Church's life of love, joy, generosity, and forgiveness, Paul says, "Be careful to do what is right in the eyes of everyone" (Rom. 12:17). Believers' gentleness and grace are to be evident to all people (Phil. 4:5; Col. 4:5-6). Paul urges them to work hard "so that [their] daily life may win the respect of outsiders" (1 Thess. 4:12) and to devote themselves to doing what is good for all people (Titus 2:7-8).

So the witness of the Church spills over into public life, demonstrating the comprehensive scope of salvation in the age to come. Paul calls the New Testament Church to become involved in the public life of their nation and to seek its welfare. In Philippians 1:27-2:18, Paul discusses "the obligation of Christians to 'live as citizens' in the world of politeia [the public life of the state] in a way that is worthy of the gospel."[1] By being visible and involved in the life of the surrounding culture while avoiding its pollution and pervasive idolatry, Christians will "shine . . . like stars" "in a warped and crooked generation" (Phil. 2:15).

The Coming of the Lord

Paul's letters are charged, as we have seen, with the tension between the already and the not yet. Though the kingdom of God has entered human history, its fulfillment awaits Christ's return. The kingdom is real in the present life of the Church, but the Church's anticipation of its future completion is its great hope, a hope that motivates the people of God to growing obedience while living in the present evil age.

Continuing the Early Church's Story

The last we hear of Paul is that he is in Rome, living in his own rented house while he waits to be put on trial. Though under house arrest, he is free to welcome all visitors: "He proclaim[s] the kingdom of God and [teaches] about the Lord Jesus Christ—with all boldness and without hindrance!" (Acts 28:31). Here Luke draws to a close his story of the Church's mission in its first decades.

It is fitting that Luke's second book should end here, with Paul still vitally engaged in the missionary task given him by God on the road to Damascus, because the story of Acts has not ended. It must continue until Jesus himself returns to bring it to completion. The work was begun by Jesus and his disciples, is carried on by the early Church after his ascension, and then continues to spread throughout the Roman Empire by the efforts of Paul and others. It is

> **In this story we too have a part, for we are invited— urged—to become a part of the story of the Church, to follow Jesus and continue the kingdom mission in the steps of his earliest followers.**

moving toward completion even now, as you read these words.

In his Gospel, Luke told the story of "all that Jesus began to do and to teach" (Acts 1:1). In the book of Acts he tells how Jesus' followers carry on that work in the early days of the Church. In this story we too have a part, for we are invited—urged—to become a part of the story of the Church, to follow Jesus and continue the kingdom mission in the steps of his earliest followers.

Scene 2: And into All the World

British theologian N. T. Wright invites us to imagine that scholars have found a "lost" Shakespeare play. Although the play originally had five acts, only the first four acts and the first scene of Act 5 have been found. A company of Shakespearean actors are given the play and asked to work out the rest of Act 5 for themselves. They immerse themselves in the culture and language of Shakespeare and in the part of the script that has been found, and then improvise the remainder of the play, allowing their performance to be shaped by the trajectory and the characters of the original.

> Consider the result. The first four acts, existing as they did, would be the undoubted "authority" for the task in hand. That is, anyone could properly object to the new improvisation on the grounds that this or that character was now behaving inconsistently, or that this or that sub-plot or theme . . . had not reached its proper resolution. This "authority" of the first four acts would not consist in an implicit command that the actors should repeat the earlier parts of the play over and over again. It would consist in the fact of an as yet unfinished drama, which contained its own impetus, its own forward movement, which demanded to be concluded in the proper manner but which required of the actors a responsible entering in to the story as it stood, in order first to understand how the threads could appropriately be drawn together, and then to put that understanding into effect by speaking and acting with both *innovation* and *consistency*.[2]

This analogy may help us to understand how biblical authority can shape our own lives. The biblical drama of redemption unfolds in five acts: (1) creation, (2) the fall into sin, (3) Israel's story, (4) the story of Jesus Christ, and (5) the story of the Church, leading to the consummation of God's plan for redemption—Act 6, which is not yet complete.

We also know that the "author" of the story, the divine "Playwright," has given his own Spirit to the "actors." Given the trajectory of the story as it has been told to this point, and especially knowing that we have been entrusted to perform the continuation of Act 5—the mission of Jesus in the church—how are we to live our lives today? How can we play our part so as to allow the story to move forward toward the conclusion God has already written for it?

According to Wright, it takes consistency and innovation. Consistency means we can't just write our part of the story, participate in our act, as though nothing happened before us. Those first four acts have "authority." We immerse ourselves in those earlier acts to understand them so well that we can live consistently with them. But it also takes innovation. We can't just repeat verbatim what has already taken place as though it were a computer program. The characters are set, the patterns of behavior are well defined, the direction is clear. Now we live out the rest of the story in our own time and place with creativity and faithfulness, leaning toward the return of the King and the coming of his kingdom.

The story of the Bible stands behind us thousands of years in time and (for those of us in North America) half a world away in distance. The biblical accounts of how all these different people struggled to live faithfully in their distant times and places may seem to have little to do with you and me. But that's not the way it is. The world of the Bible is our world and its story of redemption is also our story. If our lives are to be shaped and formed by Scripture, we need to know the biblical story well, to feel it in our bones. Further, we must also know our own place within it—where we are in the story, and how we live it out in our lives.

What Time Is It?

Brian Walsh and Richard Middleton have suggested that our lives are shaped by the answers—explicit or implicit—we give to four great questions:

1 *Where are we?* What kind of world do we live in?
2 *Who are we?* What does it mean to be human?
3 *What is wrong?* What is the fundamental problem with the world?
4 *What is the remedy?* What will fix the problem?[3]

N. T. Wright adds a fifth question:

5 *What time is it?* Where are we at in the story?[4]

These are the questions answered by whichever story about the world we adopt. If the Bible forms the basis for the whole of our lives, we must find the answers to the five great questions in its expansive story.

We have seen the biblical drama of redemption unfolding in five "acts": creation; the fall into sin; Israel's story; the story of Jesus Christ; the story of the Church. All this is leading to the consummation of God's plan of redemption in the sixth act—an act not yet complete. We also know the Author of the story. Now, given the trajectory of the story as it has been told to this point, and especially knowing that we have been entrusted to perform the continuation of Act 5, how are we believers to live today? How can we play our part so as to allow the story to move forward toward the conclusion that God has already written for it?

A Light to the World: Continuing the Mission of Israel

Thus far in the biblical story we have followed an overarching plot that includes the histories of Israel, of Jesus, and of the early Church. Israel was called to be a light to the nations. When she failed, it was Jesus who picked up that mission, accomplishing the salvation of the world. He then commissioned the Church to continue his mission, and the early Church began to do so. All three parts of this story are significant for us, for we are now called to continue in the mission of Israel, the mission of Jesus, and the mission of the early Church.

God promised to make Abraham a great nation and to bless all nations through him (Gen. 12:1-3). The nation that would issue from Abraham was to embody God's original intentions for humanity in the creation and thus to be a channel of redemption to the nations (Ex. 19:3-6). From the beginning, God's redemptive work had as its purpose the recovery and restoration of his good creation. So Israel as a community must embody a redemption as wide as creation itself. As long as Israel was obedient to this calling, it would be a light to the world. The attractiveness of its life would draw nations to God. Today, Israel's mission to be a light to the nations has become our mission as the worldwide church of Jesus Christ scattered throughout the world (1 Pet. 2:9-12).

Introducing the Kingdom: Continuing the Mission of Jesus

Though Israel largely failed in its calling to be a light to the nations, Jesus did not fail. He fulfilled God's purposes for Israel, then (after the resurrection) gathered a community of his followers and charged them with the task of continuing what he had begun (John 20:21). We are part of that community, whose task is to continue in Jesus' mission.

> **Jesus' mission centered in the coming of God's kingdom, the restoration of God's rule over all creation and all of human life.**

As we have seen, Jesus' mission centered in the coming of God's kingdom, the restoration of God's rule over all creation and all of human life. Though some Christians today believe that Jesus came to enable us to escape this creation and live eternally in an otherworldly dwelling, such an understanding of salvation would have been entirely foreign to Old Testament prophets, to first-century Jews—and to Jesus himself. Salvation is not an escape from life in creation into "spiritual" existence; it is the restoration of God's rule over all of creation and all of human life.

Christians have also misunderstood salvation as merely the restoration of a personal relationship with God, important as that is. Salvation goes much further: it restores the whole life of humankind and ultimately of the non-human creation as well to God's original intention in creation. Biblical salvation embraces this grand scope.

The scope of our own calling is to witness to that salvation. In his words Jesus announced the kingdom, and in his actions he demonstrated that the kingdom had come. He welcomed the marginalized and formed a kingdom community, taught by precept and example how to live faithfully within that community, and suffered for its sake as he challenged the idolatrous culture of his time. And he prayed for the kingdom. All of this shapes our mission today as we follow Jesus.

But our own cultural situation is quite different from that of first-century Palestine. So we need to carry out the mission of Jesus with imagination and creativity. "Jesus did not set up a rigid model for action but, rather, inspired his disciples to prolong the logic of his own action in a creative way amid the new and different historical circumstances in which the community would have to proclaim the gospel of the kingdom in word and deed."[5]

Bearing Faithful Witness: Continuing the Mission of the Early Church

The New Testament gives us both the example of Jesus' own kingdom mission and that of the early Church as it follows Jesus, bearing witness to all he has done and said (Acts 1:8). While Jesus himself concentrates on gathering "the lost sheep of Israel" (Matt. 15:24), he sends his Church out to extend that mission among all nations. The disciples must make known the good news of the kingdom everywhere, among all peoples, and then the end will come (24:14).

With the coming of the Spirit, the Church experiences a foretaste of the salvation of the kingdom: the kingdom "banquet" has been prepared by the work of Christ, but it waits for a future time, when all the guests have been assembled (Luke 14:15-24). Yet those who follow Christ have already begun to taste the power of salvation. As the Church enjoys this foretaste of the banquet to come, it becomes the prime exhibit of what the future kingdom will look like. Think of a movie trailer, a few minutes of actual footage from a film not yet released. This preview is shown so that the potential audience can catch a glimpse of what the film will look like once it is released. One important function of the Church is thus to be a preview of what the future in God's kingdom will be.

The early Church communities in Jerusalem and Antioch established a healthy pattern of witness to God's kingdom, devoting themselves to Scripture, prayer, fellowship, and the Lord's Supper, to build up their new life in Christ (Acts 2:42-47; 11:19-30). As a result, these communities did actually become effective previews of the coming kingdom of God, attracting a great many new converts (2:43-47). Because there was ample evidence of God's grace in their lives, these Christians attracted others to themselves. Beyond this local witness, the Antioch church also sent Paul and Barnabas off to take the gospel further away, establishing witnessing communities of believers in many new places across the empire (13:1-3). Thus the Church was then (and should be now) characterized by its zeal for witness nearby and missions far away.

Witness characterizes the meaning of this time period in God's story. Yet this could easily be misinterpreted: "Christian witness" could be reduced to mean only evangelism or cross-cultural missions. While these are important parts of the Church's mission, they are not the whole of it. When we grasp that the salvation of the kingdom restores the creation—all of it—we see that witness to God's kingdom must be as wide as the creation itself! To "witness" truly will mean to embody God's renewing power in politics and citizenship, economics and business, education and scholarship, family and neighborhood, media and art, leisure and play. It is not enough just to carry out personal evangelism in these areas of life. Our whole lives—the way we live as citizens, consumers, students, husbands, mothers, and friends—witness to the restoring power of God. We may suffer as we encounter another equally comprehensive and competing religious story trying to shape our culture. Nevertheless, a broad mission is central to our being.

Living in God's Story Today

We have travelled far together through the biblical story. Perhaps by now you have begun to share our vision of how God is at work in the world and in people, shaping both it and them into the great kingdom that has been God's plan from the beginning. But if each of us truly has his or her own place in the story, what place might that be? And how does this view of God's vast kingdom help us to find our place within it? In the next few pages we will try to illustrate how the lives of individuals can become caught up within the biblical story by means of two stories. These stories are completely true, naming men and women who have found interesting ways to be involved in God's ongoing work in the world.

> Gary Ginter once thought God wanted him to become a cross-cultural missionary. Instead, God led Gary into a life of service in the world of business.

Gary Ginter once thought God wanted him to become a cross-cultural missionary. Instead, God led Gary into a life of service in the world of business.

A founding partner of the Chicago Research and Trading Group (a pioneering futures and options trading firm, "the envy of the industry" according to the *Wall Street Journal*), Gary went on to become chairman and CEO of VAST Power Systems and a principal in three other commercial companies. In the course of his remarkable career, he has established more than twenty other businesses—some of them service-industry enterprises in needy communities around the world. By any standard recognized in the business world, Gary Ginter's work has been successful.

And yet Gary himself refuses to define "success" by the traditional measures of profit and power. For him, success in business as in all of life is defined in relation to the coming of God's kingdom. In Gary's own words, anyone called to live out the implications of the biblical story in the world of business will be a "Kingdom Professional":

> Kingdom Professionals do not define success in terms of money, job or status. They do not seek to maximize their income or their security or their status, or to advance their careers. Instead they seek to maximize their impact on the people and places to which God has called them. They measure success by their contribution to what God is up to in their neck of his woods. They see themselves as successful to the extent they are doing what God has called them to do, in the place to which he has led them, in such a manner that their giftedness can be well utilized. Nothing less will suffice; not the shallowness of status, not the ephemeral illusions of wealth, not the corrosive effects of power. What matters to Kingdom Professionals is that there is congruence between their daily lives and the further inbreaking of God's Kingdom where they live and work.[6]

To be involved in business, making that a part of one's life lived out of the biblical story, one must be a "stewardly entrepreneur," a careful guardian of the opportunities, talents, time, and money given by God, and dedicated to witnessing to his coming kingdom. Gary says that God has called him to make money, to live on as little of it as possible, and then to give the rest away. Acting on these principles, he has been able to establish a number of "kingdom companies," missionary corporations, especially in cross-cultural settings. These companies are in business not so much for the sake of generating profit as for the sake of providing employment and producing goods and services where they are most needed. Many countries that have closed their borders to traditional mission agencies and the preaching of the gospel will welcome such Christian entrepreneurs or "tentmakers." The business itself becomes a potent witness to the living reality of God within the lives of his faithful people.

In addition to setting up these "kingdom companies," Gary has also been involved personally and financially in Circle Urban Ministries, an organization that meets the needs of low-income families in his own neighborhood, an economically depressed area of Chicago.

Evangelism, missions, sacrificial giving, promoting mercy and justice in his own neighbourhood and in poorer countries around the world—all these are important parts of Gary Ginter's witness to the reality of God's kingdom. But as important as they are, they are not at the heart of the matter.

At the center of Gary's life is his faithfulness to God's purposes in the world of business. Gary understands business to be a good part of God's creation, developed in response to God's first command (Gen. 1:28). Business enterprises can play an important and positive role in God's world. One way to love our neighbor is by providing necessary goods and services in a stewardly way. Gary witnesses to God's good intention for business by placing love for his neighbor, stewardship of God's resources, and justice ahead of profit. He strives toward the ideal of a "kingdom company," a business enterprise shaped by the biblical story. Such a business can bless the lives of its own employees and the lives of their families, suppliers, and customers. To set such a goal for a company is difficult at a time when the idolatrous profit motive drives much of the traditional world of business. Faithfulness to God's purposes in business, Gary has discovered, may lead to suffering, both in financial loss and in reputation. But this is what we should expect in our witness.

In our second story we meet Peter and Miranda Harris, both passionate bird-watchers.

Is there a place in God's kingdom for the gifts of a passionate bird-watcher? Peter and Miranda have found that there is. An assistant pastor in a Church of England, Peter was exploring possible mission work in Tanzania when God showed him and Miranda quite a different plan for their family. Driven by their love for God's creation and especially for birds, Peter and Miranda, their three small children, and another English couple moved to Portugal in 1983 to establish A Rocha ("the Rock"), a Christian conservation organization. It was rare then to hear of Christians who were truly concerned about the environment.

But the biblical story makes it clear that God deeply loves the non-human crea-tion and has made humankind its guardians and stewards. This part of the bib-lical story moved the Harris family to act.

At that time, Portugal lacked both committed Christian ecologists and field study centers. Fragile habitats along the country's southern coast needed to be protected. One estuary in particular, a stopping point for large numbers of migrating birds, became the focus of the work. The Harrises and their staff undertook field studies to learn migration patterns, to count birds, and to sur-vey the species in the area. This data was then compiled in formal reports to be shared with national conservation lobby groups. Peter's book *Under the Bright Wings* describes the early years of the organization and some of the struggles they faced. But the hard work paid off: the government of Portugal has now granted environmental protection to the estuary near *A Rocha*.

The field center at *A Rocha* is unique in its community emphasis. People from widely differing backgrounds and levels of skill, from rookies to PhDs in ornithology, come to help collect data and to learn about the area's ecology. And from among this group, brought together at first only by their common love of birds, *A Rocha* has become a true kingdom community that also draws people to Christ. People of many different backgrounds have found a welcome at the field center in Cruzinha, where everyday activities range from technical fieldwork to conversations about theology. Sometimes people from "the outside" will ask about this "Christian" element of *A Rocha*. In these words from *Under the Bright Wings*, Harris answers: "We saw no distinction between the . . . field work and the . . . times when we could talk about Jesus with students who were staying in the house. The former [was] not secular, and the latter were not spiritual. All were undertaken out of worship and obedience, and all mattered to the Creator and Redeemer of the world."[7] When approaching the work of ecology with the goal of serving God by understanding and caring for his creation, it becomes an act of worship and obedience, a way to witness to his inbreaking kingdom.

As God works through the gifts and inclinations he himself has given the staff of *A Rocha*, the fieldwork has thus become an opportunity for witness. Visitors see the glory of God revealed through creation and through the life of a com-munity rooted in Jesus Christ. Harris writes, "As the field studies at Cruzinha developed, we . . . gave time to talking together about the ways in which they were formed by our life in Christ. It was necessary to make this a conscious exercise, because we found the instinct to compartmentalize went very deep in all of us. Only as time went on did it become less studied and more natural."[8]

Some twenty years ago, when *A Rocha* was founded, a handful of people came together to plant a seed. God has since caused that seed to grow and flourish. Today *A Rocha* has become an international organization that works in thirteen countries.

Living in Hope: Straining toward What Is Ahead

We know from Scripture that one day "every knee [will] bow . . . and every tongue acknowledge that Jesus Christ is Lord" (Phil. 2:10-11). We know too that one day all of creation will be restored. We look toward that day with hope, rooting our lives deeply in the gospel so that we can begin to make the kingdom known in our own communities even today. We live in hope, eagerly anticipating and straining toward what is ahead (3:13-14).

> Hope is a settled conviction about the future, a conviction that gives meaning and shape to life in the present.

Hope is a vital part of the faith that must shape our mission today. Hope is a settled conviction about the future, a conviction that gives meaning and shape to life in the present. We can see this in many everyday situations. If, for example, you enter a university in the hope of one day becoming a doctor, that hope will shape your life, directing not only your choice of courses but also dictating the time and effort (and money) you devote to your studies. Thus the whole of your life will take on a new look, a new focus, because of your hope for what the future will bring.

The same pattern is evident—but on a much larger scale—where our ultimate hope of the revelation of God's kingdom is concerned. What you and I believe to be the goal of history will give particular significance and form to our lives today. If we recognize that we have been called to provide our world with a preview of God's coming kingdom, the hope of that kingdom's coming will shape all that we say and do here and now. As we are pushed forward in our mission by the impetus and forward movement that we see in Acts 1-5 of the drama, we are also pulled forward by hopeful expectation of the future kingdom to be revealed when Jesus returns (Act 6).

Thus it matters very much what in particular what we are hoping for. Yet often we fail to give explicit attention to the content of our hope as Christians, our sense of where history is headed. And because our hope is not always carefully examined, there is some danger that its content will not always be thoroughly biblical. This matters deeply, since what we hope for in the future will shape our mission in the present. What is the substance of Christian hope? What does the Bible teach about the end of history, the final act of the cosmic drama? To these questions we turn in Act 6.

Finding Our Place in the Story

1. How does the Church today measure up to the description of the churches in Jerusalem (Acts 2:42-47) or in Antioch (11:19-30; 13:1-3)?

2. Act 5, Scene 2, includes two stories of people who seek to live in the story of the Bible. Do you find these stories helpful? Why or why not?

3. How does your own calling fit in the scriptural story?

4. Since our witness as God's people should be as wide as all creation, discuss how we might be faithful to God's original intention in the following areas of our lives:

   - money
   - sexuality
   - family life
   - education
   - work
   - care for the poor
   - friendships
   - entertainment[9]

Act 6

The Return of the King— Redemption Completed

When God set out to redeem the creation from sin and sin's effects on it, God's ultimate purpose was that what was once created good should be utterly restored; the whole cosmos should once again live and thrive under the rule of its rightful King. The Bible tells the story of the progressive march of God toward this final cosmic restoration. In this final section of our book, we look at history's conclusion in the restoration and renewal of God's good creation.

The last chapters of Revelation give us a vision of what lies in store for the creation as God brings history to its conclusion. The clearest picture of God's kingdom is in the person, words, and actions of his Son, Jesus Christ. But throughout the Bible we have been allowed glimpses of where the story of God's redemption is headed through briefly opened windows on God's ultimate intention for creation.

The End of the Story

In the last chapters of Revelation (especially 21:1-5) we see God's final purpose unveiled. John is allowed a vision of a new heaven and a new earth entirely cleansed of sin and evil. The old heaven and earth (in which sin and death dominated) give way to a new dominion over which the Lord rules. The Holy City, God's heavenly dwelling place, the "new Jerusalem," descends from heaven to earth. This suggests the renewal of God's order for the earth to show that God's kingdom has come and his will is forevermore to be accomplished on earth.

A loud voice from God's throne proclaims,

> Look! God's dwelling place is now among the people, and he will
> dwell with them. They will be his people, and God himself will be
> with them and be their God. He will wipe every tear from their eyes.
> There will be no more death or mourning or crying or pain, for the
> old order of things has passed away (Rev. 21:3-4).

The physical reunification of heaven and earth dramatically pictures restored
peace and harmony between the Creator and the creation. God comes to dwell
on the new earth with humankind, removing sin and all its effects. There is
no more sickness, pain, or death because the relationship between God and
humankind has been healed. God is once again as close to us as in the days
when he walked with Adam and Eve in the garden. Relationships among human
beings too have been healed: love reigns. The whole of human life is purified,
and even the non-human creation shares in this liberation from its former slavery to sin and death. Here is the stunning goal and destiny of the biblical story,
the true story of the whole world: a renewed creation—healed, redeemed, and
restored.

Though this vision of the new creation climaxes the last book of the Bible,
most of Revelation is not concerned
with the future. Rather, it gives us a
glimpse into God's purposes throughout history and in our own time, those
purposes which are leading to precisely
this conclusion. Much of the Bible
shows us the history of humankind on
earth and especially the experiences
of God's people. In this final book,
the curtains of God's heavenly throne

> **Most of Revelation is not concerned with the future. Rather, it gives us a glimpse into God's purposes throughout history and in our own time.**

room have been pulled back and we are allowed to see the spiritual battle that
has been shaping our world's history all along, a battle we could not see from
our own earthbound and historically limited point of view.

John writes to a small community of believers in Asia Minor who are suffering
terribly under Roman persecution. It must have seemed to them that they were

facing the forces of evil all alone. But John sees—and reveals to his readers—that behind the local opposition to the gospel being faced by this first-century church lies Satan's own constant and implacable hatred of Christ and his people. The little church in Asia Minor is fighting a minor skirmish in the ongoing cosmic spiritual battle. But of course they cannot see the vast scope of the war between God and Satan. So the message of Revelation comes to these frightened people: God will triumph. Those who are faithful in his service will share in the ultimate victory. Even though at present the outcome of their own battle may seem doubtful, Jesus firmly controls all that's happening in the world.

John opens the book of Revelation with a startling vision of the exalted Christ. He then explains that he has been told to record both what is now taking place in history (in his own time in the first century) and what will take place in the future (1:19). But first he is called to encourage seven representative churches in Asia Minor to remain faithful to the gospel in the midst of their suffering (ch. 2-3). Then John is allowed to see the throne in heaven from which God rules in glory and splendor (ch. 4). Twenty-four elders (symbolically representing the whole people of God—the Old Testament nation of Israel and the New Testament Church) and four living creatures (representing all of creation) bow before God and worship him.

John then sees a scroll with seven seals representing sovereign control over the direction and goal of the history of the world. When this scroll of God's purposes is finally opened, evil will be vanquished and God's people (whose names are written in the scroll) will share in his salvation (ch. 5). An angel asks, "Who is worthy to break the seals and open the scroll?" (5:2). That is, "Who is able to direct history to its goal? Who can conquer evil and accomplish salvation?" At first no one answers the angel's question. John begins to weep bitterly, for he sees that if no one can direct the course of history, humankind is trapped in a meaningless round of evil, suffering, pain, and death. An elder comforts John, inviting him to look again, to see an immensely powerful lion that has triumphed over its enemies and is able to open the scroll. And when John looks through his tears he sees not the regal lion but a pitiable blood-smeared lamb, looking as if it has been slaughtered. The victory of God has been accomplished not by a warlike lion but by the Lamb whose life was given on the cross.

As the Lamb takes the scroll from God, a hymn of praise begins with the twenty-four elders, is taken up by thousands upon thousands of angels, and at

last is chanted by every creature in heaven and on earth as they fall down and
worship the Lamb, saying,

> You are worthy to take the scroll and to open its seals,
> because you were slain,
> and with your blood you purchased for God
> members of every tribe and language and people and nation.
> You have made them to be a kingdom and priests to serve our God,
> and they will reign on the earth. . . .
> Worthy is the Lamb, who was slain,
> to receive power and wealth and wisdom and strength
> and honor and glory and praise! . . .
> To him who sits on the throne and to the Lamb
> be praise and honor and glory and power,
> forever and ever! (Rev. 5:9-10, 12-13).

In a series of vivid images the remainder of the book of Revelation reveals
Jesus—the exalted Lamb—opening the seals and guiding history to its final purpose: God's full and complete reign over all creation. Judgment and salvation
fall on the world as the crucified Victor opens the seals and unrolls the scroll of
history. John shows that the true action of history has always been this spiritual
battle, which, though normally hidden from human perception, is now revealed
to him in a series of vivid images. Though the images are intricate and at times
both puzzling and frightening, their general meaning is clear: God is the one
who, through his beloved Son, directs the course of history. God's purposes will
be accomplished; God's kingdom will come. This is the glorious concluding
image of the renewed heaven and earth shared in Revelation 21-22.

Imagine the comfort and hope that this book must have given the small, suffering church to which John was writing. Though they may be small in numbers and weak in influence, and though they must for a time continue to suffer
under the awful power of Rome, their cause is not hopeless, for they are allied
to the winning side. They follow the one who sovereignly rules history, the one
who will crush all opposition to his kingdom. They too will share in Christ's
victory.

Events Preceding the End

Three major events will usher in the restoration of creation and the arrival of God's kingdom in its fullness: Jesus returns; the dead are raised bodily, some to share in the life of the new creation, others to endure final wrath; and the world comes before Christ to be judged.

Unfortunately, these end-time events have often stirred fruitless controversy among Christians. Too much attention has been given to what God will do, how he will do it, and especially when he will do it. As David Lawrence reminds us, fixing our attention on such things is a bit like becoming obsessed with the nature, strength, and frequency of the birth pangs when we should be thinking about the baby![1] Though the "labor pains" of end-time events can be fascinating, we must give due attention to the new world to be born out of them. And so our focus in these last few pages is on the "baby," that new world which is even now waiting to be born.

A New Creation: The Restoration of All Things

Revelation 21 is a vision of a creation completely restored to its original goodness. Revelation does not give us a picture of Christians suddenly transported out of this world to live a spiritual existence in heaven forever. The biblical story does not support the idea held by many Christians that the goal is to go to heaven when we die. John's vision in Revelation—indeed in the whole New Testament—does not depict salvation as an escape from earth into a spiritual heaven where human souls dwell forever. Instead, John is shown (and shows us) that salvation is the restoration of God's creation: a new earth. The climax occurs when the "new Jerusalem" (God's city and dwelling place) "[comes] *down* out of heaven from God" (Rev. 21:2). The redeemed of God will live in resurrected bodies within a renewed creation free from sin and its effects. This is the kingdom that Christ's followers have already begun to enjoy in foretaste.

> Salvation is the restoration of God's creation: a new earth.

This concept of salvation as the restoration (rather than the destruction and remaking) of creation implies significant continuity between the world we know and the world to come. Yet the Bible also suggests some elements of discontinuity. It appears that between our present life and the life to be revealed there may be both continuity and discontinuity. Much will be familiar to us; some will be strange.

This restoration of the creation will be comprehensive: the whole of human life in the context of the whole creation will be restored. Too often our view of the future has emphasized solely the salvation of individual persons apart from the full creational and relational context in which human beings live their lives. Often the whole of the biblical story seems to revolve around "me." Yet the vision of Revelation—indeed the whole story of the Bible—leads us to look forward in hope to a creation restored to wholeness. Every facet of it is to be brought back to what God has, all along, intended for it. And within that glorious fullness and perfect wholeness, there is a place for us.

Redemption is both cosmic and personal in its scope. Human beings were created to enjoy fellowship with God within the world God made. In tempting Adam and Eve to rebel against God, Satan sought to thwart God's plan—and succeeded, at least to the extent that sin and its effects now touch all of creation. But when God set out to deal with sin and its ruinous consequences, his plan was to destroy the enemy of his good creation, not to destroy the creation itself. To destroy what he had made would concede a tremendous victory to Satan. The story of the Bible moves instead toward a conclusion in which God's restorative work will utterly undo all of Satan's mischief.

Throughout Scripture, God's kingdom is depicted as a place and time of cosmic restoration. In Old Testament prophecies God says, "See, I will create new heavens and a new earth" (Isa. 65:17; cf. 2 Pet. 3:13; Rev. 21:1-5). After Jesus conquered sin on the cross and returned from the grave in triumph over death itself, Peter proclaims the good news in Jerusalem, saying "Heaven must receive [Jesus] until the time comes for God to restore everything, as he promised long ago through his holy prophets" (Acts 3:21). Paul also emphasizes the universal scope of God's redemptive work: "For God was pleased to have all his fullness dwell in [Jesus], and through him to reconcile to himself all things, whether things on earth or things in heaven, by making peace through his blood, shed on the cross" (Col. 1:19-20). Just as nothing in creation remained untouched by sin after Eden, so nothing in creation can remain untouched by God's redemption after Christ's victory on the cross.

The comprehensive scope of God's redemptive work means, for example, that the non-human creation forming the context for human life will be restored to what God has intended for it all along (Isa. 65:17-25; Joel 2:18-27). Paul says that the non-human creation, which for so long has shared in the misery of humankind's fall into sin, is now looking forward to the coming renewal (Rom. 8:19-21).

A comprehensive redemption also means that human cultural development and work will continue. The cultural achievements of history will be purified and will reappear on the new earth (Rev. 21:24-26). There will be opportunity for humankind to continue to work and develop the creation—but now both the stewards and the earth itself will have been released from the burden of sin.

So even here we do not come to the end of the story. God's one true story of the whole world will continue throughout eternity, for such it must be for a story told by an eternal and loving God.

I Am Coming Soon!

The marvelous imagery of Revelation 21 and 22 directs our gaze to the end of history and the restoration of the whole of God's creation. John ends his book with the promise, repeated three times (22:7, 12, 20): "Look, I am coming soon!" He exhorts his readers to stand firm in the faith and warns those who remain outside the kingdom to become part of it, inviting all who find themselves "thirsty" for the salvation of God revealed in John's visions to come and drink freely of the water of life. Jesus is coming soon. All who believe and hope in Jesus, as John the apostle did, will echo his own response: "Amen. Come, Lord Jesus."

Notes

Preface

1 Bob Webber and Phil Kenyon, *A Call to an Ancient Evangelical Future* (2006). The Call can be found at the following website: http://www.ancientfuture-worship.com/afw_wkshps.html.

2 *Our World Belongs to God: A Contemporary Testimony* (Grand Rapids, Mich.: Faith Alive Christian Resources, 2008), par. 18. This can be accessed at http://www.crcna.org/pages/our_world_redemption.cfm.

3 N. T. Wright, *Jesus and the Victory of God* (London: SPCK, 1996), pp. 443, 467-472.

4 N. T. Wright, "How Can the Bible Be Authoritative?" in *Vox Evangelica*, 21, 1991, pp. 7-32; *The New Testament and the People of God* (London: SPCK 1992), pp. 139-143.

5 H. Richard Middleton and Brian Walsh, *Truth Is Stranger Than It Used to Be: Biblical Faith in a Postmodern Age* (Downer's Grove, Ill.: Intervarsity Press, 1995), p. 182.

Prologue

1 Alisdair MacIntyre, *After Virtue* (Notre Dame, Ind.: Notre Dame Press, 1984), p. 210.

2 MacIntyre, *After Virtue*, p. 216.

3 Lesslie Newbigin, *The Gospel in a Pluralist Society* (Grand Rapids, Mich.: Eerdmans, 1989), p. 15.

4 N. T. Wright, *The New Testament and the People of God* (London: SPCK, 1992), p. 40.

5 Lesslie Newbigin, *A Walk Through the Bible* (Louisville: John Knox Westminster Press, 1999), p. 4.

6 Wright, *The New Testament and the People of God*, pp. 41-42.

7 Questions adapted from Brian J. Walsh and J. Richard Middleton, *The Transforming Vision: Shaping a Christian World View* (Downers Grove, Ill.: InterVarsity Press, 1984).

Act 1: God Establishes the Kingdom—Creation

1 Gerhard von Rad, trans. John H. Marks, *Genesis: A Commentary* (Philadelphia: Westminster, 1961), p. 50.

2 Von Rad, *Genesis*, p. 51.

3 John Walton, Victor Matthew, and Mark Chavalas, *The IVP Bible Background Commentary: Old Testament* (Downers Grove, Ill.: InterVarsity Press, 2000), p. 28.

4 A very good place to start to reflect on the significance of the Bible's teaching on creation is chapter 2 of Albert M. Wolters, *Creation Regained: Biblical Basics for a Reformational Worldview*, 2nd ed., with postscript coauthored with Michael W. Goheen (Grand Rapids, Mich.: Eerdmans, 2005).

Act 2: Rebellion in the Kingdom—Fall

1 Eugene Peterson, *Working the Angles: The Shape of Pastoral Integrity* (Grand Rapids, Mich.: Eerdmans, 1993), pp. 82-83.

Act 3: The King Chooses Israel—Redemption Initiated

Scene 1: A People for the King

1 O. Palmer Robertson, *The Christ of the Covenants* (Phillipsburg, N.J.: Presbyterian and Reformed Publishing House, 1980), p. 4.

2 Terrence Fretheim, "Yahweh," in *New International Dictionary of Old Testament Theology and Exegesis*, ed. W. A. VanGemeren, 5 vols. (Grand Rapids, Mich.: Zondervan, 1997), 4:1296.

3 Cornelis Houtman, trans. J. Rebel and W. Woudstra, *Exodus*, 4 vols. (Kampen: Kok, 1993-2000), 1:9.

4 John I. Durham, *Exodus*, Word Biblical Commentary (Waco, Tex.: Word, 1987), p. 263.

5 William J. Dumbrell, *Covenant and Creation: A Theology of Old Testament Covenants* (Nashville, Tenn.: Thomas Nelson Publishers, 1984), p. 80.

Scene 2: A Land and a King for God's People

1 See Michael W. Goheen, "Charting a Faithful Path Amidst Postmodern Winds," in *In the LambLight: Christianity and Contemporary Challenges to the Gospel*, ed. Hans Boersma (Vancouver: Regent College Publishing, 2001), pp. 17-31, where the postmodern condition is interpreted as the failure of the Enlightenment idols of reason, science, and technology.

Act 4: The Coming of the King—Redemption Accomplished

1 Hans Kung, *On Being a Christian*, trans. E. Quinn (Garden City, N.Y.: Doubleday, 1976), p. 91.

Act 5: Spreading the News of the King—The Mission of the Church

1 Bruce W. Winter, *Seek the Welfare of the City: Christians as Benefactors and Citizens* (Milton Keynes: Paternoster Press, 1994), p. 82.

2 N. T. Wright, "How Can the Bible Be Authoritative?" The Laing Lecture 1989 and the Griffith Thomas Lecture 1989. Originally published in *Vox Evangelica* 1991, 21, 7-32; available online at http://www.ntwrightpage.com/Wright_Bible_Authoritative.htm.

3 Brian J. Walsh and J. Richard Middleton, *The Transforming Vision: Shaping a Christian World View* (Downers Grove, Ill.: InterVarsity Press, 1984), p. 35.

4 N. T. Wright, *Jesus and the Victory of God* (London: SPCK, 1996), pp. 443, 467-472.

5 Hugo Echegaray, trans. M. J. O'Connell, *The Practice of Jesus* (Maryknoll, N.Y.: Orbis, 1984), p. 94.

6 Gary Ginter, "Kingdom Professionals: An Old Idea in New Wineskins," *Paraclete Perspective* 2, no. 1 (Spring 2002): p. 8. Reprinted on http://www.tentmakernet.com/articles/ginter.htm.

7 Peter Harris, *Under the Bright Wings* (London: Hodder & Stoughton, 1993; reprinted Vancouver: Regent College Publishing, 2000), p. 117.

8 Harris, *Under the Bright Wings*, pp. 108-109.

9 An excellent source for discussion starters on these issues is "The Mission of God's People" in *A Contemporary Testimony: Our World Belongs to God*, par. 41-54. This can be accessed at http://www.crcna.org/pages/our_world_missions.cfm.

Act 6: The Return of the King—Redemption Completed

1 Cf. David Lawrence, *Heaven: It's Not the End of the World! The Biblical Promise of a New Earth* (London: Scripture Union, 1995), pp. 9-10.